Love the Mess

Robin Emmerich

Austin, Texas

re books. -- 1st ed.
ISBN 978-1-64184-365-2

I was exhausted. My brain hurt, my heart ached and I couldn't put my finger on what it was- I was just tired. With a husband, two kids and a full-time job, I rarely took time for myself. I mean, who are these people that have time to meditate and go to yoga and volunteer and take field trips with their kids every weekend? When do they get laundry and grocery shopping done and do real life things? My life was chaotic and I wasn't happy. I yearned for something more.

I walked into Robin's office and sat on her sofa. She asked me what I hoped to get from our meeting and all I could think to say was "Peace. I just want peace in my life." I didn't have a clue how to get there. Robin promised to take me down a path to find that place of calm that I desired. She also told me that it wouldn't always be easy. I was okay with that. I wanted the result more than anything and I was willing to put in the work to get my positive outcome.

Robin has given me the tools I need to grow from within. She has educated me on how to get my power back. She has shown me how to look in the mirror that reflects each of our souls. She has awakened a creative side within myself that I forgot existed. She helped me get rid of the need to always be in control. She taught me how to make decisions with my heart. To breathe. And just be kind. There's only 24-hours in a day and somehow, by practicing what Robin has taught me, I have more time in a day to give myself. I'm a better wife, a better mother, and am now self-employed. I take care of myself and meditate every week, and I volunteer at several organizations. I'm able to get it all done- the things that I envied people for having the time to do and the real life things. I have peace and harmony in my life. Every. Single. Day.

— LAURA W.

I was lost. I was unfulfilled. I was unhappy. I was going through the motions but wasn't fully engaged or present. That was before working with Robin. After our first meeting I could instantly tell she had a gift. Robin helped me change my life. With her guidance and support she helped me find passion for life again. She gave me the tools that can be used in all aspects of life, and for this I'm forever grateful.

— COURTNEY F.

"As a wife, and mother, and giver, I was living a reactionary life: adapting to whatever those around me needed or wanted. It was like I was waiting for others to validate my reason for being.

Experiencing some shocking personal loss I experienced how unsustainable this really is and the inner chaos it creates. Robin helped me to slow down my reactionary process, listen to my heart, and learn to articulate what I really wanted in life. I began to "show up" and be present in my relationships, unafraid of shame or rejection because I found acceptance within. It's an amazing freedom because I am living with this inner peace and freedom, I am more open to joys and gifts from the universe: I ended up buying a home I never thought I would have; found the love and support of a partner that I was not expecting, and genuinely enjoying my life with gratitude and less stress."
— MARY S.

I am delighted to respond to the wonderful message in Robin's first book, one of many that I am sure she will write. Her message is filled with hope, inspiration and possibilities for improvement in the life of every reader.

In describing Robin as a student and client I find no better way to describe her than to use the sunflower as a symbol of her overwhelming growth and progress in life. One might think of her as a sunflower seed, starting sprouting at a very young age, anxious to experience the earth and its surroundings. Once the sprout took roots it began to soak up the moisture and sunshine and push its roots deeper into the ground and grow the leaves it needed to experience more sunshine and growth. There were times when the weeds around the plant almost smothered it but with tenacity it kept pushing toward the light. There was wisdom in that seed that gave it determination. It knew that buried within its cells there was an inner strength that would fulfill its mission if it kept its head focused on the light. The growth continued as it reached out in all directions with its leaves, motivated by an inner urge to be more. The destiny of that plant was always there encapsulated in the cells and provided for by its Creative Force.

Then one day that plant began to form a pod of seed at the very top, the part that reached up to the Light for sustenance. Hundreds of seeds, clones of that one seed containing the essence of the strength, love and inner wisdom that were needed to continue planting the truth of life for all those who would plant the seeds and allow them to grow.

Robin is scattering those seeds of inspiration, love and wisdom so that others may be the recipient of the growth that she has experienced. She believes because the principles of life worked for her and she wants to scatter those seeds so that others may be aware of the wisdom and strength that lies within them. I applaud her on her journey of Light.

Coletta Long, Ph.D.

FOREWARD

In about 250 BC, Aristarchus of Samos, an ancient Greek astronomer and mathematician who presented the first known heliocentric model (placed the Sun at the center of the known universe with the Earth revolving around it). During his lifetime and for over 1700 more years, people were taught and believed that the earth, not the sun, was the center of the universe. His work was largely ignored.

In 1543, Nicolaus Copernicus published On the Revolutions of the Celestial Spheres. In which he also described the studies he had performed to prove Aristarchus' theory that the sun, not the earth, was the center of the universe.

Galileo Galilei, now considered by many to be the father of science, supported the work of Copernicus. The matter was investigated by the Roman Inquisition in 1615, which concluded that heliocentrism was "foolish and absurd in philosophy, and formally heretical since it explicitly contradicts in many places the sense of Holy Scripture." He was tried by the Inquisition, found "vehemently suspect of heresy", and forced to recant. Pope Paul V instructed Cardinal Bellarmine to deliver this finding to Galileo, and to order him to abandon the opinion that heliocentrism was physically true. On 26 February, Galileo was called to Bellarmine's residence and ordered:

... to abandon completely... the opinion that the sun stands still at the center of the world and the earth moves, and henceforth not to hold, teach, or defend it in any way whatever, either orally or in writing.

He spent the rest of his life under house arrest.

This true story about "science" continues to this day.

I am trained as an ophthalmologist and finished my eye residency in 1968 at the University of Texas, Southwestern Medical School/Parkland Hospital in Dallas and Harvard Medical School/Mass Eye and Ear Hospital in Boston. Thus, I have been an ophthalmologist for fifty years! I was trained to remove the cataractous lens from the eye and patients had to spend 2-3 weeks in bed after the surgery and wear very thick glasses. I went to Europe and was trained how to insert plastic lenses inside the eye after cataract surgery so that normal glasses would suffice. I was then subjected to an inquisition by the Chairman of Ophthalmology at Southwestern Medical School. I was told that no one so stupid as to put lenses in eyes after cataract surgery had any business teaching ophthalmology. (See Pope Paul V edict to Galileo above.) I was fired from my teaching position at the medical school and told that all of my patients that had surgery by me had to be inspected by one of the chairman's henchmen. I refused. However, I was forever banished from teaching at my medical school (like Galileo's house arrest) even though it is now malpractice not to put lenses in eyes after cataract surgery!

I found that giving the elderly cataract patients general anesthetics often made them confused. Their children would often tell me, "Mom's never been the same mentally since her surgery." I developed a beveled incision in the eye that was water-tight so that the patients could move normally after the surgery and we used local anesthetics so that the patients could go home immediately after the surgery. I was again forced to undergo an inquisition by the leadership of the medical staff at the hospital. They claimed I was putting my patients at risk by sending them home immediately after surgery because they still had medicine (local anesthetic) on board. Thus, we admitted all of the day's patients to the recovery room, gave them their anesthetic blocks and let the recovery room nurses discharge them as recovered from their anesthetic. On their way back to their rooms, we had them stop in the operating room and have their surgery. They were then immediately sent home. The hospital punished me by making it difficult to get operating time. I purchased a building nearby and opened the first outpatient eye surgery center in Texas. Later, I was asked by the state to be the chairman of the adhoc committee that wrote the rules that govern outpatient surgicenters in Texas.

I could share many other stories of my experiences of the resistance of those in power to the advancements in science. But this story is not about me. It is about being willing to consider, with an open mind, things that don't seem to fit your current paradigm/belief system.

We have all heard of the "mind/body connection" but few can tell you what that is. They simply say that if you have emotional baggage, you will get sick. Counselors of many types, religious and secular, have attempted to talk people out of their emotional baggage, but that has been only marginally successful. One of the reasons is that few can tell you the difference between a memory and an emotion. How and why are they recorded differently in the body. Where is the information recorded? Why is an event emotional for one person and not for another?

It seems that these recordings are made in what has been called the subconscious mind whereas we use the conscious mind during our daily life. The conscious mind cannot change the recording in the subconscious so "talk therapy" of the usual counselling type doesn't have much effect.

Then there are the religious considerations. Was there a life before this one? Is there a life after this one? What things do we bring with us to this life when we are born? What effects are imprinted in our subconscious during the nine months that our mothers carry us? Do mother's hormones, anxieties, fears, etc. during this time also get recorded in the growing baby? And then there is the question of whether we live multiple lives, one after the other.

Most people either don't think about these things or simply dismiss them out of hand. I developed a technique to cure eye pressure problems in glaucoma patients and I had no side effects from the procedure. The Medicare experts told me that if I cured another glaucoma patient, I would be banned from ever seeing another Medicare patient. (I was interfering with the profits of the glaucoma eye drop companies). However, the patients where I had cured one eye and was not allowed to cure the second eye were very unhappy. They simply had experienced the "miracle" that the experts said could not happen.

This book by Robin Emmerich falls into that category. Many will scoff at its concepts and dismiss it out of hand. They will say it isn't scientific (meaning it doesn't fit into their current way of thinking). But those that experience the physical and mental relief it offers will beg to differ.

As one of my mentors, Dr. Malcolm Ing says, "Results always trumps theory!"

Read the book and experience the effects of this method. You may find that the earth really isn't the center of the universe despite what Pope Paul V said and your current teachers/professors say.

Jerry Tennant, MD, MD(H), PScD

CONTENTS

Your Transformative Journey Starts Now: *A heartfelt note just for you:*

I know you. I have been there. The struggle you are hiding under that perfectly manicured handshake or behind that flawless hairstyle. I know about the aching you feel despite the smile on your face and the amazing shoes on your feet. On the outside you look like you have it all and you've tied it all up in a beautiful package, but in reality, there is something missing and it is eroding you from the inside. Maybe you have a similar journey to mine; you are climbing or have climbed that corporate ladder and get to see the view from the top. You followed the steps you thought you needed to in order to have a "perfect" or "happy" life. You did what you thought you were supposed to do to be "successful." When I got there, something stopped me. I was not connected or happy. I was in literal pain and needed to change.

The anxiety that can manifest behind the daily life that you need to keep running can be toxic. It can creep up on you while doing the laundry, helping the kids with homework, going to the gym, or driving to work. As you start this transformational journey, these things will not magically change. They will still exist as you work through them, but it may make you feel like you are not doing this thing right. Or maybe you cannot see that changes that are happening because so many of the emotions that are no longer serving you are going on. The fact is that life continues to unfold, bringing stress and distractions with it. But when you awaken your desire to be happy and live up to your highest potential, you uncover an amazing support system along the way. It should not be (but often is) surprising that there are countless others transforming every day along with you. You are not meant to do this alone- and you do not have to!

Often, when these feelings of anxiety or despair creep in, it is because you are missing tools to work through them. You need a collection of phrases and techniques to help you get through the tough times a little bit easier and with a little bit of joy. What has brought you here today is the recognition that the "old" way of approaching life is not working. The social-media-surface and judgments and gossip over coffee are not filling the gaps any longer, but rather are making them deeper. The more you live in this superficial existence, detached from your true self, the more suffering and confinement reveals itself. And many times, instead of recognizing that happiness and peace are available, you think that there is something "wrong" with you. To be clear: there is nothing wrong with you, you are just missing the tools to live your purpose like you are meant to.

We are all here to bring something to the world. We are all meant to live in peace according to our higher purpose. We are meant to be loved and share love to all those around us. You are not meant to be alone, and the truth is that you are never really alone. When you connect with yourself, a beautiful thing happens; you find the strength to use your authentic voice, share your struggles, and break free from the external "expectations" you were trying to live up to. And as you bond within, and expansion takes place around you: you help elevate yourself and those around you to authentically live.

As you begin to turn the pages, remember that it is so much more than just a book to pass the time. It is your guide to changing your life, over and over again, when you need to let things go, grow your potential, or nurture relationships. Use it one time to unlock your creativity and then again to find your voice at work. Pick up again when you need to work through a challenging time in your relationship and a fourth when you want to deal with a situation with your children. No matter what life throws at you, in any arena, the tools and techniques in these pages are your tools for the journey. Use them when needed.

The pages of this book are filled with easy to follow, step-by-step instructions on how to transform your life. Love the Mess is intended to help you through whatever you are going through right now, and offer lasting support for other things that bubble up over time. You will even find guided meditations to help you discover inner peace and guidance. This book is the ultimate tool for constant, life-long change that always nudges you back on the journey to your authentic self. It helps you realize how truly amazing you are, despite all the mess! After all, what if this mess is what it is really all about, anyways?

Get ready to discover how quickly you can enact positive change in your life.

Sometimes it is hard to see or feel in the beginning, but the wheels you set in motion just by beginning this transformation is life-lasting. The meaningful relationships, connections, decisions, and interactions you have moving forward are proof that you are living the life you are meant for. It is remarkable and I cannot wait for you to experience it!

This book is my invitation to join a life filled with purpose and happiness. It is my invitation to join my quest to empower and spread love all around the world. Just by picking up this book, you are starting the journey for universal change that the world needs right now. You are ready to be fulfilled and happy in everything you encounter. You cannot experience this until you recognize you are ready for it. Today, you are ready!

Do not worry, this doesn't need to consume your life. Life is still going to march on while you are transforming, and it is crazy enough without having to try to stop for a self-discovery break! Follow the chapters of this book and the instructions on the pages, in the order they are presented at first, you will be able to start change in all areas of your life. Later, when you have learned the tools and need to return to the instructions, feel free to pick and choose where you need to go. Your inner GPS will tell you what tools you need to help you. Trust in it! You'll find that you will open opportunities for yourself because you have shifted your focus to what you need to be fulfilled. Take this time to grow and expand. Try not to treat it like another line on your to-do list, but rather a personal space to connect with yourself and what matters in your life. It is this time that will show you what is a priority and is not, and that alone is invaluable.

Through the path outlined in this book, I share with you the stories that have been shared with me over the past decade as well as my own personal experiences so you can see how the steps have worked with others. These tried-and-true methods have helped me embrace the life that I am meant to live, as it has countless other women around the world. So, now is the time to take a deep breath, give yourself permission to do this, and let's get going! Your one decision to start this book has already started your transformation; congratulations! You are changing yourself and the world around you. Thank you for joining me on this life's gift and making a difference. You are an inspiration to so many others already!

With all my love,
Robin

The Best Way to Read This Book:
Do not skip this section!

Before I go on any further, it is important for you to know that this manual for life is presented to you in a way to learn a series of techniques for dealing with the craziness in life while still pursuing your passions and purpose. My intention is for you to read and work through it from start to finish at least one time before using it as a go-to guide for life's challenges later on. I am certain that after working through this book the first time you will have enough tools to help you drive forward unleashing creativity, passion, and capabilities you never knew were inside. But, if you feel called to jump to a certain chapter or section of this book, then follow your "gut" and go there. The Soulwork is attached to the end of every chapter for you to experience. No matter where you are in the process or what you are working on, if a particular Soulwork sounds intriguing for you and you want to tackle it, then go for it. Same goes for the journal prompts.

This is not your typical self-help, life's path, old-school novel. It is not a quick and dirty guide to getting ahead in your workplace or making the "man of your dreams" fall in love with you. It is a tool for helping you fall in love with yourself and all that you are capable of. And of course, it is revealing those things to you so that you can see how valuable it is for you to embrace them. You need to accept your authentic self before anyone else can. Allow yourself time while going through these chapters to discover these truths.

This book has three primary sections. The reason for these sections is to provide you with specific guidance and examples for everyday situations, personal relationships, and professional growth. Each chapter focuses on helping you identify and work through each of these situations so you no longer feel "stuck," anxious, unhappy or afraid. In the first chapter, I encourage you to work through the content and instructions. It is the foundation of your transformation and provides invaluable tools for resetting your emotions and opening space for you to move on. This section is the foundation of my practice with my clients and something I am very passionate about. It is the best place for everyone to start on their transformation. At the end of this first section you will have a variety of tools that will specifically help you in all areas of your life.

When you finish the first section you can "choose your own adventure." If you are coming to this book for help in your personal life, move on to the second section and its guidance. If you are seeking assistance in the workplace, go right to section three. Section two deals with challenging personal relationships and how to navigate loved ones and your own path. Section three is about dealing with relationships and situations that arise professionally. No matter which path you choose to explore, you will end at the conclusion and finish with the same final Soulwork at the end of this book.

When you follow the guidance of this book in the way it was intended, you will enjoy life lived according to your highest purpose. It will reveal to you possibilities and talents that you never knew existed before, and the awe and beauty of this will allow you to feel the connection to life even more.

You will start showing up in your own life in ways you never imagined before, and it will be amazing!

In these pages is the map to clearing away the things that no longer serve your true self, making a path clear for you to make relationships and situations real. It is all possible, but it will take effort. And compassion mixed with a bit of patience. It will be fun and maybe even awful at times. Sometimes you will fight against the exercises while other times you will be jumping to do them over and over. Remember the reason you are doing this and what you are looking to get from it. Everything on these pages is a technique I use to live the best life I can, and it is something I wish for you and everyone in the world to do as well.

With These Words, I Invite You to Join the Journey of Authentic Truth

Most of us want to know the truth and then at the same time, we run from it.

I want to connect with you on a deeper level, no matter where you live or what is happening in your life right now. Bound by the bonds of truth, I believe we can connect with our purpose, while growing our connections within and to those around us in a positive and meaningful way. This connection doesn't need to take away your energy and efforts in any way, but rather provide a clear path for you to devote your time to those things that really matter to you.

Loving your mess is more than trying to deny or cover up the mess. It's about understanding and embracing the mess of life with peace and happiness, knowing that this crazy whirlwind you live in can be beautiful, if you let it become what it is meant to become for you. You are here because you have sensed that there is more to this life than the glossy cover-up that you have been conditioned to wear. There is more to success than a great job or "perfect" family. It is time to stop stifling who you are to fit this "mold" of expectation and to embrace who you are meant to be. It is time to accept that you live in a world full of chaos and mess, and that is ok! You can get excited about the possibility before you and the journey that the Universe has in store for you, if you just get out of its way and let it lead you there.

You don't have to travel this path alone, and there is a community of other women out there who believes there is so much more to life than the surface situations. You add value to the lives around you and can show up to life more fully and more purposefully than ever before when you begin transforming your perspectives to the craziness of life. As you begin this book, you choose the path to follow your highest potential and the path intended for you. You agree to forgive yourself when life gets in the way and old habits break in your progress. You choose to let go of expectation and live your true life. You allow yourself time to feel the experiences of life and then guide yourself back to the direction that is serving you to your purpose.

Before you go any further, make the commitment to yourself now that you are ready for a radical new way of approaching your life. Commit to yourself to nurture your highest potential and connect with your highest self so you can live the best life you are meant for. Once you have made this commitment,

You are ready to begin!

INTRODUCTION

Life is messy. No one is perfect. But, what if the mess is actually necessary? The best thing that could ever happen? A gift.

No matter if you want to attract a fulfilling relationship, create a successful business or find freedom from fear and doubt, the Emotional Reset Method (ERM) can help. It is your "how to" in navigating the mess.

"What do I want?"
"Who am I?"
"What am I here for?"

These are questions from the soul. The problem is that our society often pushes us to create a sustainable career and lifestyle before asking ourselves these questions. In our scattered attempts to make the external version of our life and career look appealing and successful to others, we find ourselves alone and exhausted. Rarely do we ask ourselves;

"How do I feel?"
"Do I love my life?"
"Am I happy?"

I help women facing these dilemmas each and every day. There are countless modern, professional women who feel lost and overwhelmed. The process of ERM has taught women all over the world how to release the blocks that prevent them from manifesting their dreams and discovering their innate power to create the life they wish to lead—real-life solutions to live a more fulfilling life.

With the solid foundation of knowledge and experience, the powerful breakthrough technique I developed was born from asking myself these very questions. But more than that, I answered them with an honest and open heart. What did I find? That true happiness is only achieved when we take that honest look within to understand who we are and what we really want.

Life will always lead us in the right direction. The Universe will bring you where you need to be. And until we experience it in our own lives, this can be hard to understand and accept. This is because we need to become clear and in touch so that we can be led. An amazing series of events have transpired to lead to this book, for example. I guess you could say that this really started back when I was 9 years old, needing to be perfect and coming to a misguided conclusion that I was here to change the world. Next was the death of my father, which led me to work with my mentor, Dr. Coletta Long, a pioneer in the field of regression. After years of working and collaborating with Dr. Long, she passed down her world-renowned training program to me to carry on her legacy. Her methodology contains over sixty-five years of experience and knowledge on the subconscious mind.

Now combining my ten years of a transformational journey into the heart with Dr. Long's legacy, I bring ERM, or the

Emotional Reset Method, to you. Working one-on-one with clients using this method, I have had the privilege of observing their new and improved wellbeing, emotional understanding, and, most importantly, their purpose in life. I have seen people discover hidden talents, become free from emotional binds, reignite their personal relationships, and thrive in their professional settings. Each discovery and transformation is unique and beautiful, which has made the concept of creating this manual a challenge. How could I possibly present this method in a manner that would help you transform your life when each person's experience is so personal? Just like you, I go to the basics of the methodology and release my emotional and creative blocks to free my method for presenting this material to you!

This process is different from others because it accesses and taps into the light within your heart, as well as aligning the mind, body, and spirit. Through this book, you'll experience the power of the mind and heart with this transformational roadmap along with personal accounts of how they are applied to real life. Sharing my personal journey, perspective, and client stories of how to reach your highest potential provide you with an opportunity to know that you are not alone and you can live a heart-centered approach to life. You hold the power to set yourself free.

Imagine that your freedom is deep-set in your emotional response to life. Multiple times a day you respond emotionally to situations, just like everyone else in the world. It is a natural human response. The emotions you have suppressed or have not faced can build disguised walls against others and leave you feeling separated from the people around you and from your authentic life. Yet, when you resolve emotions from the past and learn how to navigate your present emotions, you have the opportunity to be happy and in touch with your best self. When you are in this state, you can connect with others and relax in knowing you are living the life you are meant to live.

You'll learn how to be more mindful, connect to your heart, and make choices based on your true desire in your heart rather than on unconscious, external factors that bombard us all. Using the Emotional Reset Method, you can experience a lasting change in a relatively short amount of time.

A Quick Note on Emotional Responses

To begin your transformation, you need to know what an emotional response really is and the power our emotions hold. When something occurs in your life, big or small, you respond to it emotionally before you even have a thought about it. It happens instantly and internally. It is a physical response to any situation that you did not anticipate, like or want. The important distinction is that your emotions occur before you have time to even think about the situation. Allowing your emotions to form your response means you halt your ability to think about the situation. If you stop yourself from addressing the emotion you block your ability to think or communicate openly. You erect an indistinguishable wall between you and this situation. But this wall keeps out everything else as well, including positive emotions! Instead of helping you, this response actually makes you feel less connected to others and to yourself. You can feel misunderstood, alone, and afraid. We often perceive that it is external, a person, place or thing that is causing the response, when it is in truth, it is an internal disconnect.

My Story of Being "Stuck"

Like my clients, I have personally experienced the pain of feeling "stuck" and living life simply going through the motions. As I checked my goals off my list, I felt empty, despite my professional achievements as an executive with a national healthcare company. Indeed, the more I strived for what I thought was a perfect life, the more of a mess I found the rest of my life to be in. In fact, I spent almost a decade after my father's death on autopilot. On the outside, it looked as if I had everything. On the inside, I was dying my own slow death.

I'd love to say I grew up in a normal American environment in Austin, Texas, yet what is really normal? I guess it was kind of like a fairy tale.

- My dad worked demanding hours at a Fortune 100 company.
- My mom stayed at home cooking, cleaning, shuttling us to school activities and smothering us with love.
- I was set to graduate top of my class and attend Baylor University to pursue a degree in Psychology.

That is, until my dad went to the doctor for a pain in his shoulder and was diagnosed with cancer.

It was said to be 97% curable, so in just about every way, I continued to live in the fairy tale. Until the unexpected happened on Valentine's Day, 1997.

After 9 months of chemo and a final surgery to remove the cancer, my dad was one of the 3% that didn't make it.

I felt more pain, shock and grief than I ever knew was possible. The fairy tale was over, the happy ending never happened. Life lost its meaning.

And it stayed that way for a decade, until something happened that forced me to wake up.

FACING THE LAST TIME, FOR THE FIRST TIME.

A series of events, including a car accident and an attempted break-in to my apartment forced me out of the trance I was living in — and into an acupuncturist's office.

I knew something in my life needed to change, but I couldn't figure out what it was.

That's because from the outside looking in, everything was perfect.

So I chose a university closer to Austin that my sister had been attending instead of Baylor, but it was still a great school and a great education.

During that education, I changed my major from psychology to business.

That led to me running a healthcare company that was incredibly successful.

I also found myself in a long-term relationship with a wonderful man.

Living in Austin, I was surrounded by my family and life-long friends, wonderful human beings, all of whom supported me in everything I did.

I worked out, and kept a healthy, sculptured and manicured physical appearance.

To anyone watching, I was thriving.

But I felt a deep sense of emptiness, anxiety, and soul-shaking questioning about if there was more to life.

My acupuncturist suggested that life had brought me to this place of questioning to heal the unresolved grief from the death of my father ten years prior.

With a sense of curiosity, I ventured onto a path of self-discovery and growth devouring every possible book on near death experiences, grief, and sought mentorship on how to wrap my mind around death and find the more that I was searching for.

What I discovered was not what I had expected.

I had little connection to the God that I had prayed to as a child. I was raised Catholic and lived most of my life believing that God was a physical person whom I was trying to please, so as to be rewarded in life and avoid punishment. I wanted to be the good girl, do everything perfectly, and receive love from others. Based on my own experience, it proved to be a tough expectation to live up to.

As I grew, I felt increasingly removed from that parochial image of God. I desired to explore what was weighing me down psychologically so that I could find more freedom. I had been stuck in logical, rational thought processes for so long that I had to learn to release the limiting thoughts and beliefs that were preventing me from consistently tapping into my intuitive self. Everything inside of me yearned to experience a deeper connection to my higher self. I did not know it at the time, but I was about to be led to the perfect opportunity.

This endless loop led me to Dr. Long where I found the root cause of my imbalances—unresolved emotions stored in the cells of my own body, such as grief from the death of my father almost ten years earlier. The insight and release of "frozen blocks," as coined by Dr. Long, created massive changes for the better in my life and compelled me to uncover an inner world of thought, feeling, and power that has transformed my life and helped me pave the way for others to experience the same joy and fulfillment.

Through my sessions with Dr. Long, I discovered a force that connects us together as humans. Some people call this a higher power, God, Universe, Source, Jesus, Allah, Spirit, Light, love, intuition, truth, etc. I embrace whatever word you feel called to as, in my opinion, it is not *what* you name this connection as it is important to come to terms with your own *relationship*—how you *receive* guidance in your life. Take time to discover what freedom means to you.

My journey meant I became ready to understand how the Universal laws worked. My soul was ready to be free of the pain of the past, suffering that I caused and that caused me to suffer.

The subconscious mind is like a computer that has been recording every single one of our life experiences. Whether we are consciously aware of it or not, these subconscious recordings affect how we perceive and process our daily life.

The heart is a part of the body's electromagnetic field (think acupuncture) and changes with our emotions. The heart is in constant communication with the subconscious—absorbing corresponding energies and affecting how we perceive and process conflicts and challenges. The mind and heart are our connection to our own intuitive guidance.

THE LIFE-AND-DEATH CONUNDRUM: FAIRY TALES ARE REAL. SO ARE NIGHTMARES. THAT'S OK.

I received a new set of eyes to see a whole new world. A world where fairy tales, reality, dreams and nightmares co-existed.

I experienced a way of healing the candle inside of me that had turned into a huge ball of wax as each year passed after my father's death. I re-lit that candle and the ball of wax in me dissolved. The light sparked brighter and brighter and everything around me sparkled with a beauty that was beyond words.

The most painful event in my life—the loss of a loved one, and having then to also face the reality of my own death—had transformed into an event of purpose and meaning I never knew was possible.

I again felt the love my dad had always given me—and with that, I enjoyed taking the leap to leave the corporate world to become an entrepreneur.

In that quest, I helped others reclaim their lives through an inner strength they didn't know they had. That strength, I learned, came from knowing that beauty lies in every moment, every day. It also comes from discovering what it means to each of us, and to our souls, to leave behind a legacy in this world, to overcome the fear of death, and to embrace our humanity.

THE LEGACY OF A LOSS. THE BEAUTY OF WHAT WE CARRY ON.

My father's death created:

- A work/life balance program at his Fortune 100 company as it took 3 employees to replace his position.
- A non-profit created by my mom in his memory providing hand-made blankets made with love to the local chemotherapy hospitals to keep patients receiving treatment warm.
- A coaching practice helping people to transform their pain into purpose.

The beauty of death is not always right in front of us, yet it is always there.

The ones we love really never leave. When we allow ourselves to open our eyes wide, we can embrace in our hearts all the beauty that is there. We can create a legacy and carry our loved ones with us.

An Overview of the Emotional Reset Method

"There is a path toward peace, joy, and fulfillment for every person."

Intuition is another natural human response to situations. Think about a time your "gut" told you something was "off" only to find out later that you avoided a serious situation. Or you just had this "urge" or "need" to call someone to check in only to find out something was wrong in his or her life that you could help with. These are examples of your intuition working in your favor. In our society, we often are told to ignore this feeling. These moments actually allow us the opportunity to connect and experience this intuition. Recognizing your emotional barriers and detaching from past experiences and unresolved emotions is your pathway to reconnecting.

This process requires you to cultivate courage and face the avoided emotions that are keeping you detached so you can be happy and free. This process is not about forgetting; it is about discovering yourself through your past memories. You can release the power these emotions hold over you and change your perspective to live in the present emotions of your connected life. You can release your fears, trauma, anxiety, and depression. You can live the life you were destined to live and see yourself as you truly are.

The method is designed to help you navigate your emotions as they arise, release their power, and allow you to respond with love. Giving yourself permission to allow this process to be messy, to be what it is, and take the time to press the "pause" or "reset" button in your life is the most loving thing you can do. Instead of feeling overwhelmed by something out of your control you now have the tools to align your perspective so you are empowered. You can respond intelligently and calmly. This process allows you to resolve the past, find clarity in the "cycle" your life is operating in so you can break the negative patterns, revealing the life you are called to live. You will see the meaning of your life and prevent future trauma from happening. You are not blindly responding, but rather feeling and thinking clearly. Keep applying this technique in your life and you will feel whole, connected, and at peace, both mentally and physically.

Now, let's begin!

PART ONE

Learning to Love Your Mess

CHAPTER ONE

UNCOVER YOUR MESS

"The way of the Creative works through change and trans-
formation, so that each thing receives its true nature and
destiny and comes into permanent accord with the Great
Harmony: this is what furthers and what perseveres."
– Alexander Pope

You have made the decision to begin your transformative
journey. You have taken the first step toward a more connected and beautiful future. The journey is personal and
individual; you hold the power within to reach the destination
of freedom and creativity.

Every condition can be traced back to a subconscious desire that comes from an energy blockage in the soul. The
blockage is usually caused by guilt, which is itself a manifestation of fear of punishment (think about how we beat

ourselves up for what we did/did not do). Although we may not consciously feel a fear of punishment, I see this fear deeply rooted in many of my clients. To the subconscious mind, fear is energy blocking our awareness of the Light, bringing about more opportunities for fearful events in our lives.

Fear is a "frozen block" in control of our life. We need to take control of the energy and change it, thereby taking control of our life.

Developing yourself and growing your connection to your true self involves your mental, spiritual, physical, intellectual, and emotional state. Most often, a significant life event led you here to find inspiration and empowerment. Regardless of why or how you got here, the outcome is more fulfillment: at work, in relationships, your self-perception, or worldview. When you revisit this process throughout your life there is an endless opportunity ahead of you. Possibilities open up and talents are discovered. This first step is the starting point for all this, so let's get started!

To begin, you need to start asking yourself some pretty real questions and allow the emotions to surface that come with your honest answers. This is best if you do it in a quiet, private room. Ask these questions to yourself out loud and answer them the same way. Trust and write down your response exactly how they come to you. It is a discovery process. If you can, record this interview or conversation you are having with yourself so you remember everything you said and exactly how you said it. The simplest phrase or word could be what unravels your whole transformative process. You can write things down as you go, but you do not want to focus too much on the recording, but more on the dialogue unfolding.

During this discussion, we will be tuning into your thought patterns. We will uncover how you think and create a new roadmap to clear your mind. The goal? To release the emotions holding you back after you have cleared your mind! Imagine how beautiful it will be when you peel back the layer of pain or emotion that has kept you from experiencing the world in the way you are meant to!

Now, sit down; dedicate about 30 minutes to an hour; ask and answer the questions below:

- Where are you in life now? Describe the journey that has led you to this very moment in your life.

- Describe your relationship with your family. Review how you remember experiences with them. What was it like growing up? What are your relationships like now? Be clear about how each interaction or experience made you feel. Do the same for the other major parental roles in your life.

- Think about the last job you were in, whether you are in it currently, it was paid or not paid, or was decades ago. Think about the memories you had from that position. What struggles did you face while in that role, and what did it feel like to handle the experiences? Move to the job you had before that and do the same discovery process.

- How do your current relationships make you feel? Do you feel connected and free to be who you are? Are you holding back in order to please those around you and keep everyone happy?

- Think about how you want to feel. What you are wishing for as an outcome? What do you wish was a different outcome from a previous situation? This could be family related, career-related, relationship related or just your life desires. The goal of this is to discover what you are longing for.

Through this discussion with yourself you will be able to identify some key things;

1. The emotions that you experience in various situations
2. The role influential people and experiences have had on your life
3. What you wish you could have experienced and want now in your life.

To share an example of this conversation, I had a meeting with a client, Andrea. She came to me feeling lost and out of control in her life. She had previously been successful in her career and enjoyed the direction she felt everything was heading until her life directed her a different way. She was let go from her job, unexpectedly lost her mother, and moved from a bustling city to a quiet town in a remote state. Through the transition, she also had her third child and felt a mess emotionally. While she recognized that because these events all unfolded at the same time, in her mind, she accepted how things were meant to unfold. Yet, she was unaware that in her heart, she had been struggling with the transition for years.

She described her new life as staying at home with her children, trying to maintain the household, and learning how to adjust to a new city. A path she had never envisioned for herself before! She sat down for our first meeting emotional and strained. Through this process of discovery, I was able to discern that she had never allowed herself the time to experience the emotions related to any of the events she had experienced. As is often seen in today's busy and involved world, Andrea felt she had to "keep it all together" in order to keep her family and their home functioning. This meant she did not "have the time" to give to grief, anger, frustration, or sadness. For years, these emotions have sat dormant in her mind, infecting her body, while she knew in her heart what she truly desired was to be loved and to feel loved, to be at peace, and to feel that what she is doing, and who she is, was enough. These were profound discoveries and a great start to the transformation process and emotional healing.

Each person will discover something unique in this step. It is about identifying the mess and getting to the heart of the matter. It is about uncovering your blocks and freeing up space for clarity and prosperity. Your block may be personal, creative or professional. We will learn different tools to help you clear these blocks in different situations so you can live a more connected and fulfilled life in the areas you most desire. Once you complete Soulwork 1, you'll choose which direction you'll take on your journey. If you want to transform your career, follow the "Field Guide to Your Professional Purpose" path. If you are experiencing blocks in your personal life or creative outlets, find the "Clarity in Your Connection" section to help uncover how to heal your soul and become in tune with your life you are meant to live.

You've started; now keep going.

This is where you need to move on to the next step. After you have determined these emotions and situations and people that have influenced who you are today, it is time to do some

Soulwork. Before you begin on the next step of your journey, complete the exercise on the next page:

SOULWORK 1

Identify and write down 2-3 thoughts every day for 3 to 7 days. These thoughts can be positive or negative, and about anything or anyone. Just write down a few concepts that came up to go through during your next step. At this point, do not solely focus on your personal life or professional situations. Keep your recording general. We will have time to focus in on your path soon.

JOURNAL PROMPT

"Every condition can be traced back to a subconscious desire that comes from an energy blockage in the soul. The blockage is usually caused by guilt, which is itself a manifestation of fear of punishment.... To the subconscious mind, fear is energy blocking our awareness of the Light, bringing about more opportunities for fearful events in our lives. Fear is a "frozen block" in control of our life. We need to take control of the energy and change it, thereby taking control of our life."

Think back to situations or relationships that seem to repeat themselves. For example, do all your relationships end with bitter fighting or broken trust? Do your career choices tend to fizzle out, causing you to become restless and discontent? See if you can trace these repetitions back to a primary source; when did this pattern start happening?

CHAPTER TWO

THE BEAUTY IN THE MESS

*"By three methods we may learn wisdom: First, by reflec-
tion, which is noblest; Second, by imitation, which is easiest;
and third by experience, which is the bitterest."*
– Confucius

Within our thoughts lies our reality and our reality is also
molded by our thoughts. Have you ever wondered why something bothers you so deeply and yet does not affect someone
else at all? The thoughts you had in the past, even from when
you were a child when you were the most vulnerable to emotions and learning the lessons of life, are part of what is
creating your life today. The relationships you engage in, the
career path you are pursuing, and the hobbies you engage in:
all these things are based on your thoughts developed over
years. So then the question is raised; are the thoughts you recorded from your Soulwork new thoughts from an "unbiased"

reality, or are they actually tied to what has occurred from your past that you have yet to resolve?

Our consciousness reflects our beliefs. Many of them are positive and beneficial, while others can create an enormous amount of adversity for us. One of the beliefs that most often creates difficulties is the conviction that we are victims—of circumstances, of other people, of our own fate. This pattern can be referred to as the victim archetype. The concept of archetypes dates back at least to the time of Plato and his theory of ideal forms. Swiss psychologist Carl Jung developed it further to include psychological patterns derived from historical roles in life, such as the Mother, Child, Servant, Queen or Warrior, as well as universal events or situations, including Initiation or Death and Rebirth. Jung believed that in addition to what he called the personal unconscious, which is unique to each of us, "there exists a second psychic system of a collective, universal, and impersonal nature that is identical in all individuals." This he called the collective unconscious, which he believed was inherited rather than developed and was composed mainly of archetypes.

Although archetypes are impersonal patterns of influence that are both ancient and universal, they become personalized when they are a part of your individual psyche. Although Jung mentioned just a limited number of archetypes, his ideas have been expanded further in recent years by a number of spiritual teachers, chiefly Caroline Myss. In her body of work including Sacred Contracts, Myss identified a group of "survival archetypes," which include the saboteur and victim.

These archetypal patterns are often unconscious and may include beliefs that we have internalized from our parents and others. For instance, we may believe that we are the victim of our environment in the form of chemicals, crime, accidents, earthquakes, and floods; our work atmosphere, government policies, place of residence, heritage, genetic make-up, family behavior, relationships, spouse, siblings, parents, children, employer, friends, religious concepts, God, and the devil.

All of these victim categories are secondary. The real driving force of the victim archetype can be found in the words Worthlessness, Helplessness, and Hopelessness.

- **Worthlessness**: We usually believe in what we think we deserve. If you think, "I'm not worthy," you will act in such a way that you will not be.
- **Helplessness**: We possess limiting thoughts, reasons not to try, and a lack of inner strength. Ideas such as, "I am not capable" or "I don't have what it takes" dominate the mind.
- **Hopelessness**: If you feel, "It's impossible, there's no hope, no one will help, there is nothing left for me, no one cares, so why bother?" you probably won't bother.

The key issue is *deserving*. If you feel undeserving and are experiencing Worthlessness, Helplessness, or Hopelessness, guilt is often the underlying cause. Locating the cause of the guilt is paramount. Releasing the frozen blocks relating to that guilt allows you to feel that you deserve to succeed in your life and you begin to love yourself more. In order to change your beliefs, you have to want to change and be open and receptive to the process. It is then that you can see a new perspective on a situation or relationship and understand the core root of the conflict.

When we release the fears of life and begin to be aware that we are the creators of our lives, we are no longer victims. My mentor always spelled the word Guru— "Gee, You are You!" When we live as the victor and create happiness for ourselves, we create it for the entire Universe. We are molding the energy of the Universe into good and serving the world.

"Moments from your past design the illusion you see that you call your 'present reality."

Through transformation, you can begin to appreciate the opportunity you have in front of you to begin shaping the "future" version of yourself. Taking the time now to see the past for what it truly is, the influence that has led you to this place means you can now discover what you need to change so you can grow.

This revelation will open your mind for this next step: *think* about things differently from the past so that you can *live* a different future.

Through inspirational stories, written and verbal exercises, and visualizations, you will learn how to connect your subconscious mind to the light within your heart so that you can tap into your intuitive guidance system. This step is the first key to learning how to see past outside expectations and the "I should—I shouldn't" thoughts and listen to your inner voice.

Let's take a look at your Soulwork. What thoughts did you write down and what phrasing did you use? What one or two thoughts were the most surprising or impactful to you? Write them down here:

1. _____

2. _____

Now, let's talk about those thoughts.

What was happening when you had this thought? Was it a positive experience? Did it hit you seemingly out of nowhere? Is there a common theme in your thoughts? Is it fear of rejection, doubt, parenthood, success, being worthy or enough? See if there is a common link between everything that you wrote down, including the two listed above.

The more you can uncover about the circumstance of your thoughts the better. Look inside and find the core root of this thought. This is a way for you to find clarity. You are moving from just experiencing these thoughts to a deeper understanding of them.

We can't attract our dreams and desires when we are not clear on what they are. When we become aware of our own thoughts in our mind and the desires that we hold in our hearts, we naturally light the path ahead. To know what we really want, we connect the mind and heart.

The thoughts of the mind and the heart are very subtle, yet both contain the power to create in every moment. The easiest way to discern the thoughts from our mind is to notice the thoughts that feel judgmental and constricting. The thoughts of the heart feel hopeful and expansive. As we start to focus on what feels good, we draw more of it to us. What is most important is carving out space in our day to take time to listen, develop the skill of listening and the inner strength to follow our own guidance. It is easiest to start small, such as what to eat, rather than ending a relationship. The mind and heart will be clearer in time and trust will begin to build.

Annie was a client of mine that came to me very confused and uncertain about her life. She explained it as if she was walking around every day with a furrowed brow and squinting eyes, trying to figure out what was going on, and always feeling like she was missing the punchline. She had been let go from a career that was in line with the path she had been following since graduating high school and recently moved to a new city in an attempt to fill the void but was not fulfilled. She felt lost and aimless. During our first session, I had uncovered a tumultuous relationship with her mother. We examined her thoughts over a seven-day span.

What I found interesting is that Annie organized a project each month to do with her children to empower and teach them lessons such as empathy, goal setting, and strength finding. One of the projects was to create a strengths board for each person and assign a superhero to them. This way, they can see their own power and remind them that superheroes use their strengths to help others. Her kids chose the invisible woman as her superhero. She didn't think anything of it until she saw the visual image of the invisible woman and was struck how she felt it was appropriate that her kids viewed her as invisible. Inside, she felt like no one saw her as a person and didn't feel valued for all she did for the family. She felt that her needs were at the very bottom of the "totem pole." Her Truth sat at the bottom of the family's obligations heap, and try as she might, she could never get enough cleared off on top to address what she needed.

As we explored this thought, we began to expose more of her fear. She kept coming back to her fear of not being a good enough mother, always comparing herself to how she viewed her own mother's presence in her life. She was able to reflect on how powerful this mental thought was negatively impacting her heart. Her heart knew that she was enough, that her family does value her contributions, but her mind kept telling her she was not appreciated. As we continued, she explained that she often felt that she was not asked what she wanted by her family when making choices, but in reality, they do ask her. Simple day to day questions like, "Where do you want to eat tonight?" or "What do you want to do this weekend?" are examples of her husband wanting to do things for her and recognizing her wants and needs. Instead of taking these opportunities, she would brush them off and say, "I don't care." or "I've been making decisions all week long, I don't want to choose anything else. You pick." She had fallen into the habit of ignoring her heart and keeping herself in the downward cycle of being "invisible."

So much came from this one thought. So much can come from your thoughts, if you sit down and take an honest look at where it comes from. Are your thoughts self-sabotaging your desires? Is your mind overpowering your heart because you have let it run on autopilot for too long? If you are like Annie, they are.

Asking yourself the deeper question:

Visualize/ imagine connecting to the highest part of you.

"_____, (insert what word feels right for you, I often use the word Universe to imagine the light within me connecting out to the stars in the sky) **is it in my highest good to (believe)**   **?"**

Fill the blank with your mental thought.

For Annie, it was "Dear God, is it in my highest good to believe that I am invisible?" Yours may be feeling enough or feeling self-doubt or fear of rejection. Take the voice that you uncovered in your thoughts, ask the highest part of yourself if it is in your highest good.

Watch how your body responds to the question.

This is your guidance. Is your body tense or does it feel free? A tension reveals that you reject the question and it is not true to your heart. If you feel light and expansive, this is your truth.

For example, when Annie asked herself if it was in her highest good to feel invisible and not a good mother, she felt tightness in her lower abdomen and her body tensed up. When I asked her why she thought her body responded this way, she first thought it was because she didn't really want to know the answer. I explained this was her heart that was connected to her truth. The answer was no.

The final step in the process is to give you the free will to accept or reject this answer.

Annie could choose to accept the answer of "no" or she could continue to feel invisible and not a good enough mother.

When you accept your heart's true desire and your connection to your higher power, you can release the power of negative mental thoughts and begin following your heart's emotional guidance.

It is now your turn to step into this process.

In this example, I will call it "Universe" but you can change that to your name for your higher power. To begin, you need to find a quiet place to connect with your higher power. Sitting comfortably, close your eyes and take a deep breath. As you inhale, bring your awareness to your lower abdomen. Exhale. On your next inhale bring your awareness to your lower back. Exhale. On your next inhale bring your awareness to your stomach. Exhale.

Now you are ready to ask yourself the question:

"Dear Universe, is it in my highest good to

_____?"

As you ask yourself this question, observe how your body responds. Do you feel light and expansive or tight and churning? This is your response. Trust your body. Yes or no.

Now, choose to accept or reject this guidance from your own truth. Do you accept the yes or no you received? If you accept the response, you can remind yourself of this or ask the question again if the thought appears again in the future. Bring yourself back to your connection and hear the truth again and again as you continue to accept the guidance.

Remember, your thoughts and reactions to your present situation are something created from your past experiences and thoughts. This means you have the choice and ability to change them, but only if you want to. The key is in listening to your truth and choosing to accept your desire to change.

As you continue to practice connecting with your higher self, you will be able to "tap" into your link easier and faster.

Now that you know how to tap in and listen, you are ready to move forward.

SOULWORK 2

As a thought occurs to you, continue to write it down or connect to the moment and ask for your heart's truth. Choose to accept or reject your highest truth. Do this over the next three to seven days. Record some of the thoughts you explored and the feelings you had when you received your own truth. Have these available to you when you begin your next step.

JOURNAL PROMPT

"When you accept your heart's true desire and your connection to your higher power, you can release the power of negative mental thoughts and begin following your heart's emotional guidance

Name a time when you felt a deep connection to your Higher Power within. For example, think about a time when things just seemed to "go right," or when you felt that you didn't even have to try to get things moving in the right direction. What was it that you were doing, who you were with, etc.? Write down the details of the situation.

CHAPTER THREE

THE MESS IN THE MIRROR

*"There are two ways of spreading light: to be the candle
or the mirror that reflects it."*
– Edith Wharton

Expanding on the possibility that our reality is designed by our thoughts, we can begin to open to the possibility that our perception of the people around us— the ones we love and the ones drive us crazy—are also a reflection of our thoughts. Is it possible that our perceptions or thoughts of others are actually covering the truth of the beauty of that person? If we change the way we think by accepting the guidance of the Universe and releasing our blocked emotions, will our judgment of others and ourselves change as well?

You'll find out by experimenting with the possibility and see what unfolds!

What you'll discover is that it's not that the person will change, what changes is how *we see* that person. Your perception is a direct reflection of you, so naturally, you will judge based on your own self. This means the judgments you have in others is actually a judgment you have about yourself. (Take a deep breath here and take it all in with love and compassion). The challenge with self-judgment is that it is an internal dialogue you may have been having for so long that it is hard to recognize. It is easy to think that this view is the only view of who you are and these negative thoughts will feel "normal."

To turn the tide on judging yourself and others, you want to reveal "the man behind the curtain." Exposing your own judgments of yourself and others for what it is will allow you to let it go.

This step is one of the most powerful. It can be hard to look at yourself in this way, and when you take the time, to be honest with yourself, you take a great leap forward in transforming your life. It will become easier and the adage, "The truth will set you free" will become your best friend.

In this chapter, you will learn how to hold the image of a mirror in the mind's eye. Through combining visualization with personal inquiry exercises, you will be primed to see a new perspective on current life conflicts and challenges.

Through releasing the illusions in my mind, I saw a new path that didn't require years of suffering. In learning how to identify what my mind said and what my heart wanted, I learned to follow the path of the heart, the path to love. When we look into a mirror, we see a direct reflection of ourselves and we also see the opposite. Life will reflect the same. In learning to use the mirror of life—looking directly at people, places, and things in front of us and then turning that experience back onto ourselves, we can uncover the truth of our heart. The voice of the heart sets change into motion.

Reviewing Your Soulwork

Consider your Soulwork from the last chapter. What did you notice when you connected with your higher power? Write down one example of what you connected and discovered in your own heart's desire:

1. _____
_____
_____

When you asked your heart this question, while connected to your highest self, how did your body respond? Write down the physical response your body had to the question you asked:

2. _____
_____
_____

Finally, how did you respond to this answer? Did you choose to accept or reject the answer your heart gave you? Write down your acceptance or rejection statement: I chose to accept/reject my heart's desire to:

3. _____
_____
_____

As you understand the conversation between your mind and heart, you can begin to choose to follow your heart's desire. The heart is always your positive guide.

Continuing Your Transformation

Our life will reflect back to us our deep beliefs about ourselves. Through identifying the thoughts in the mind, we can then choose to release the belief that is not in alignment with our heart and discover a new path. This truly requires a lot of compassion and ability to take charge of what you allow into your life. Sometimes we are not ready and that is ok. Life will put the reflection right in front of us until we are ready. I cannot stress the importance of being gentle with yourself as you become more aware of your mind, heart, and discovery of the choices that have brought you to this very moment.

Imagine holding a mirror to your thoughts and judgments so that you can recognize that what you think of is a direct reflection of who you are. For example, if you think that someone is not reliable or dependable, ask yourself the tough question, are you dependable to others? Can they rely on you to follow through on your word? If you accept that you can be disappointed by someone's performance at work, is it because you recognize in him or her the ability to apply their talents more confidently to fulfill their tasks? Now ask yourself, do you feel you can apply yourself more fully to your role?

"Through the process of reflecting your thoughts back on to your own life, you will discover the truths about yourself and your own judgments on your performance."

As a leader, parent, or partner, your expectations and thoughts about how others act or perform is a reflection of how you see yourself. When you come to terms with that, you can begin to interact with them with more empathy and your heart, rather than your mind. You can begin to release fear-based actions such as attempting to control or the need for others to be perfect and allow others to live and lead. You may experience disappointment, anger, sadness, or other uncomfortable emotions, and will learn how to release these emotions as they occur.

When we look into a mirror, we see a direct reflection of ourselves and we also see the opposite. Life will reflect the same. For example, we all know someone that at some point or another is completely unhappy and everything around him/her seems to be in a constant state of chaos. If we find ourselves thinking a million different judgmental thoughts about him/her, these thoughts are like an alarm clock going off for us to see the truth—something within us is unhappy and in that same constant state of chaos. He/she is a direct reflection of our own life. If we are aware, centered and focused, we may find ourselves feeling deep compassion for him/her. This is the opposite reflection that the mirror reveals. Taking it a step further, we trust that he/she is exactly where he/she is meant to be, knowing that the state he/she is experiencing is an opportunity for growth. The same goes for our own lives. Holding the image of a mirror in the mind's eye helps to integrate this concept. The more that we can objectively visualize a physical mirror in front of us with a purpose to lovingly show us where our soul is ready to grow, the truth can more easily be seen.

Joseph Campbell calls the path of transformation the hero's journey. When we step fully into the journey, we are often required to face the shadow of the victim within and become the victor. The light of the victim is the victor.

"A hero is someone who has given his or her life to something bigger than oneself." – Joseph Campbell

As Julie navigated the path of the hero and journey from the mind into her heart, she discovered that her mind and heart were on two different pages. Her mind carried the repetitive questioning from her family and friends, "Are you seeing someone? You don't give anyone a chance." These thoughts were a direct reflection of how she felt. "I feel like a failure that I haven't found someone," I asked her what her heart wanted. "Do you want to date?" Her response, "I want to be confident in my career. I really want to date someone but I would hate for them to see me struggle." Her mind had decided that until she reached the level of success she thought would make her worthy of dating, she was off limits. Thus, unconsciously letting any man in, in fear of being "seen" and possibly "rejected." In just the thought of opening her heart to love, she felt scared. Her heart said, "I have so much love to give" and her mind immediately shouted, "They won't love you back."

Julie was shocked by how "negative" the thoughts in her mind felt. She was ready to look at the truth. Her heart spoke louder, "I want to date someone." I could feel the conviction in her statement. She felt it. She was ready to open her heart. Later that month, she met a guy that was the perfect reflection of everything she wanted in a relationship. They went on several dates, had a lot of fun and she realized what was possible. She realized that she could date and build her career. Life was not an either/or.

To be alone is to defy every universal law—nature is a cycle of death and rebirth. We are never truly "alone." Our mind is the vehicle that tells us what we think is true. Our perceptions have to be challenged. If we cannot let go and let life be, we are pushing against life. We have the opportunity to embrace each day as an entirely new experience. What happened in the past is the past. It is not relevant today. There is nothing that can withstand the pain, hurt, sadness or fear more than just being open to letting it flow and move through. To let the love in. Relationships are one of our greatest teachers. They help us see the truth, evolve, and love more deeply.

Julie carried a deep fear of opening her heart. At seven years old, her father had a heart attack and suddenly passed. Unconsciously, love equaled loss. As she looked back at her life, she began to see through the eyes of the mirror and connect the dots. She had disempowered herself with a victim mindset and was ready to learn more. She had attracted the perfect opportunity for change. She took a clear, objective look at her last relationship. She had felt a need to protect and take care of the man she was dating. The mother archetype was strong in her relationship. It is often challenging to be intimate when the dynamic is more like a mother/child relationship. The mirror reflected her desire to nurture, love and protect herself. Placing herself as a priority in her life felt exciting and scary for her. Even though she had ended the relationship, she still felt a need to provide and protect. Upon seeing this reflection, her mind and heart got on the same page, this man had been a gift in her life to focus on her wants, needs, desires and attract the healthy, loving relationship she was now ready for.

This shift opened her eyes to a new way of dating. She felt grateful for the opportunity to meet a guy that in her words, "showed me that good guys do exist." Rather than fearing rejection or abandonment, Julie now approaches each date as a way to get to know herself more and have fun in the process. The heaviness and constriction that felt overwhelming for her transformed into feeling more light and open, thus attracting men more compatible with her own desires. As she felt more free to explore what was possible, she met her now husband and is due to have her first child in the next few months. Julie will enter the field of mompreneurship (yes, it is a real thing)! There is so much growth as a mompreneur!

When we are ready to be whole, we can go back into the past, experience the parts of ourselves that we are afraid of, recognize and then reclaim each of those parts. When we deny those parts of ourselves, we are not whole. The conscious mind will say "I have forgiven," for example, but the subconscious has not forgiven until you feel the love, joy, and abundance that flows from genuine forgiveness. This is wholeness. As we release these fears and find freedom from their bondage and limitations, we begin to change our perception of past events, assisting us in the release of fears, limitations, conflicts and false beliefs. We then begin to believe in something greater than outer appearances. We release judgment of others, ourselves, and stay connected to our heart. It is a beautiful moment!

Another challenge of this step is to recognize that thoughts can be a direct opposite of you. Maybe you view your spouse as undependable because you are very dependable. But as you ask yourself more about your dependability and their unde-pendability, is it because you have a need to control a situation, giving little opportunity for your spouse to help or help in the "right" way? Are you so concerned with every-thing being perfect that you do not allow them to help or give up control enough for them to do something their way?

The things in life that irritate us the most are either direct actions or habits we embody or something that highlights the habits we have that need to be examined. For example, if you become frustrated with your spouse because they are "stub-born," are you yourself stubborn? Maybe, yes, and it is time to evaluate why you are not willing to listen to other's ideas openly. What if you feel you are not stubborn? Is it possible that your spouse's firm ground that they stand on is something you are lacking, and the stance they take shines a light on the one you can now develop?

Let yourself hear your heart's desire more clearly so that you can follow its lead confidently. You hold the power. My client Melissa describes this process as a "spiritual bridge." She explained she would often do this after connecting with God and asking herself if it was in her highest good to think a certain way. When she discovered her answer, she began to look into the mirror and find out what her heart's desire truly was. She says she continues to go back to this technique over and over again to connect and look in her mirror. Melissa first came to me when her son became estranged from the family and began a relationship with someone she didn't approve of. She struggled with acceptance and love. We later reconnected and she was struggling in her marriage. Each time we would explore her fears and uncover the truth of how they were re-flecting on her relationships. Through her "spiritual bridge" she came to terms with her own needs and desires that have now led her to a new fulfilling career and new loving relationship that she now describes as her soulmate. She is happy and comfortable in her decisions because she stays connected with her truth.

Many of us go through life not knowing our own needs. When we don't know what we want, we can't ask for it. We can easily get in the habit of giving other people our power. Using your mirror to see into your mind's eye and your heart's desires helps you find what is in your highest good and feel the confidence to navigate a path that often unfolds one step at a time. Using this tool allows you to release illusions, pain, and confusion so you can find your inner desire. Not knowing our own truth, owning our worth or looking at how we manage our personal power permeates every aspect of life. Whether it is about relationships, money, love, work, or health, life will often resemble a pendulum. It will swing from the negative pole to the positive pole; one extreme to another, until truth and balance is achieved.

Practice Your Reflections

To practice, using your thoughts listed above, reflect on the thought you had written down in step 1. When reflecting on each thought, consider if it is a direct reflection of how you think about yourself or if it is the exact opposite. Record your honest evaluation:

4. _____

_____

_____

If it is an exact reflection of yourself or the opposite, connect to your higher power and ask if it is in your highest good to think this way. If you find it is not in your highest good, begin to uncover what it is you can do to change your behavior or responses to create a different reflection.

You have the tools in your toolbox now to face the truths you may have uncovered about yourself in this reflection. Take the time to release the blocks that are keeping you from responding in love and compassion to the people around you. It is an unfortunate reality that all too often we save our harshest judgments for the people we love the most. Now think about how harshly you are judging yourself! Releasing this is a powerful skill that will open up both self-love and love for your family, friends, and community. Continue to use this new tool to reflect on how you can connect and choose to live according to your highest good.

As another example, going back to my client Annie, she felt that her husband was not dependable. She had planned a weekend trip for the family and had everything packed and ready to go when he got home from work one Friday night. When he walked in the door, he told her that he forgot to call the hotel and make a reservation. She was disappointed and angry. She connected with God, asked herself if she was right in feeling disappointed that she could not depend on him, and her response was it was in her highest good. When we met for our next session, I asked her to reflect this thought onto her life and ask if she was dependable. She honestly reflected and said she was dependable. She cares for her three children, always there for them, making sure they have what they need, always is prepared, and follows through on her word as much as she can. While we talked, we explored what the exact opposite looks like. She was always dependable; making sure nothing was ever dropped or forgotten because she was always on top of it. She controlled everything in the household. She rarely delegated responsibility to her husband because of her fear of it not being done well or correctly. This mentality set her husband up for failure and of course, he would not live up to her expectations! Annie needed to reflect this thought back on to her own heart's desire to learn that what she wanted was someone to help. She never gave (or allowed) the opportunity to be helped or helped successfully.

Annie changed the way she saw the conflict and challenge in her relationship and is now able to follow her heart's desire instead of (again) self-sabotaging what she really desires. You, too, can push past your illusions created in your mind, deliver yourself from suffering, and follow a path to love.

This step is an ongoing dialogue you will continue to have with yourself through your entire life. It shines a light onto your "frozen blocks" of energy and begins to open the pathway to your true self. You are healing your soul each time you connect and this tool creates the bridge to your soul's true intention.

Your motivations, intentions, and behaviors are reflected back to you through every interaction and relationship you have with others. These interactions can be seen as "good" or "bad," the truth is that they all shine a light on your inner being. Each person you encounter is here to teach you something, just as you are teaching others. Part of that lesson is learning more about yourself as well as developing compassion for others. It is a powerful lesson; acknowledging your feelings attached to these judgments.

Now that you know this, imagine the beauty and love you can give and get! Now that you know this, you can begin practicing holding the mirror up to yourself and recognizing your reflection in others.

With this knowledge, you are ready to continue your transformational journey.

SOULWORK 3

Identify one thought each day and ask yourself honestly, "Is this a direct reflection of myself or the exact opposite?"

Write down a few of your reflections over the next three to seven days.

JOURNAL PROMPT

"When we are ready to be whole, we can go back into the past, experience the parts of ourselves that we are afraid of, recognize and then reclaim each of those parts. When we deny those parts of ourselves, we are not whole... As we release these fears and find freedom from their bondage and limitations, we begin to change our perception of past events, assisting us in the release of fears, limitations, conflicts and false beliefs. We then begin to believe in something greater than outer appearances. We release judgment of others, ourselves, and stay connected to our heart. It is a beautiful moment!"

What past experience is still causing fear in your life and is holding you back from being whole? How can you practice releasing this so you can be free?

CHAPTER FOUR

BUT FIRST, THE EMOTIONAL RESET METHOD

Even though you may want to move forward in your life, you may have one foot on the brakes. In order to be free, we must learn how to let go. Release the hurt. Release the fear. Refuse to entertain your old pain. The energy it takes to hang onto the past is holding you back from a new life. What is it you would let go of today?"
– Mary Manin Morrissey

Some memories seem to be so deeply engraved in the brain that they can haunt an individual as if he were a permanent prisoner of past experiences. One researcher asks the question: "How does the memory of a traumatic event carve its canyons and basins of memory into the living brain?"

These observations reaffirm my understanding of the "frozen blocks." Yes, we do have deeply engraved memories, but they are not limited to the brain. As (Neimark, 1995) [i]points out, researchers have verified the fact that a memory associated with emotionally charged information gets seared into the brain, to which I would add from my understanding and experience, not only the brain but into cells of the body.

Memory, after all, is what we base our sense of self off of. It builds what we feel is a solid image of ourselves. Memory is ephemeral and complex. You can even possess a "memory" that is completely false! You remember something so clearly that it has shaped your reality; however, it is something that never even happened. Research by Elizabeth Loftus showed that many people could be easily influenced by creating these false memories. Sometimes our memory "protects" us from the harm it can inflict on us, like how trauma victims block out events leading up to, during, and after an event, while other times it can "hurt" us by creating pathways in our brain and body that make us relive the emotions and experiences over and over again. For example, when we have a fear of water we constantly avoid situations with water, experiencing a sense of dread when near an ocean or lake, and even feeling the sense of anxiety when someone mentions swimming or boating.

Memories are sneaky, too. They can settle in the subconscious, influencing you without you realizing it. In extreme examples, patients with brain damage can still recall information without knowing that they are doing so. This is because the memory of those things has "hidden" away in the brain in a special place. This means our memories are primitive and multifaceted.

There is something even more fascinating with memories and the imprints they leave on our lives, both physically and mentally; it is malleable. We have the ability to change and shift the power a memory has on us. As Neimark says, "...memory carries a power that promises to utterly reshape the self." There is no single place in your brain and body that memories are stored. For instance, the memory of something is stored in an entirely different location than the emotion associated with the memory. This finding is what allows us to alter or release the power of the emotion of a memory without removing or altering the memory itself.

I have personally found both the ancient teachings and more recent science on this subject to be fascinating and at times comforting. Regardless of what information we may uncover, the knowledge is already within us, and if we listen to the inner guidance, we can hear the truth that resonates with us and separate it from what does not.

You can release these emotions for current events and past events, at any time. The tricky thing is that sometimes you will have felt that you released the power of these emotions, but because they are so complex, and stored in various parts of your brain and body, there may be multiple layers. Think back to the example of being afraid of water. The event that led to the fear of water is something you do not want to alter; it is the fear you need to address. The Emotional Reset Method (ERM) will help you take the power away from the feeling of fear. Fear is not "bad", fear can protect us and save our lives. You hold the power to not allow it to alter how you enjoy your life or stop you from participating in your life. This is why we release the stored emotions that are holding us back from recognizing the truth of it. When it comes up again, release it again.

ERM is a simple and powerful method to release the power of emotions and remove your energy blocks. It is important that you do this step after you have learned to release your judgments so that you can view your experiences without judging the emotions you feel surrounding them. Again, the event and the emotion live in different parts of your brain and body. You can choose to let the power of these go while still recalling the events. You are bringing awareness to your life with a pure heart. There are no "right" or "wrong" or "good" or "bad" emotions. There is simply a response to a situation that is either helping you live your true life or a reaction that is holding you back. If it is later, it is time to let it go.

Emotional pain is an energy that has taken the form of a frozen block; this emotional energy is no different from the energy causing physical pain and can be handled in much the same way. Let's say you feel depressed, often a feeling located somewhere in the torso area. This emotional pain can be described by many names, including emptiness, separation, anger, loneliness, sadness, or some combination. If you guide yourself through connecting with your higher power or self-hypnosis—you may discover thoughts, more feelings, words (spoken and unspoken), and even images. When you follow this energy back to the origin, you may gain access to a memory of an experience that brought about the emotional pain.

When the mind, through the thought process, is in the Theta rhythm, a deep meditation or trance, this energy can be transformed. You can release the pain through understanding, forgiveness, and a change of consciousness that can bring about an awareness of Light. The awareness of Light is the empowering tool that affects a transformation of the energy or frozen block. This process may best be described as soul-healing, partly because many of the memories come forward with the soul, and by changing the energy these destructive memories no longer go forward with the soul in their painful form. The memories may remain, but they lose their "charge" and their ability to block the flow of energy in your system. It's not unlike the way in which acupuncture uses needles and heat to remove blockages and free up the flow of vital energy, or chi, in the body.

Dr. Jerry Tennant, a world-renowned Functional Medicine physician has discovered how emotions play a role in restoring health to those with chronic disease. He describes it as that our memories and emotions are stored in the body as magnetic fields, very much like a magnetic needle writes images onto a disk in a DVD recorder. To understand how we can influence this system, we must first understand that every acupuncture circuit in the body functions at a different frequency, much like different radio stations. Now think about an orchestra. If all of the instruments are in tune, you have beautiful music. However, if one of the violins is out of tune, that is what you hear screeching above the music. Our memories are stored in the body with frequencies that are in tune with the body; however, our emotions are stored with frequencies that are out of tune like the out-of-tune violin. In order not to hear the screeching noise of the emotion 24/7, we build a wall around it so we don't have to listen to it. The problem is that the wall blocks the flow of "voltage" through that circuit, lowering the voltage to the organs that circuit powers. That is how emotional baggage causes illness—the so-called mind/body connection". Since emotions are frequencies, they can be tuned. We are fine tuning our emotions through the power of mindfulness, self-inquiry, and emotional intelligence similar to Dr. Tennant's process of tuning the emotions with scalar energy to a frequency that is compatible with the body. Thus, one can tune an emotion into being just a memory.

Think about a time that you felt stressed.

Like the type of stress where you've got so much going on that your brain ends up racing every night OR you just feel lost and don't know what to do...

Work. Parenting. Family. Relationships. Dating. The list goes on...

Life can be a slow build of tension and busyness... or sometimes it hits you all at once. You feel that weight in your chest, the heaviness in your body, those foggy clouds in your head...

I've felt it. I was working 40-50 hour weeks. Overwhelmed with clients, my work, my personal life.

No time for my relationship. No time to paint (which is my passion). No time to spend with family and friends. I had SO many projects going on that required all of my attention.

I felt like my life was in an endless whirlwind.

I was tired of it.

And then, I explored using Dr. Long's method as a tool in my daily life.

After using Dr. Long's method for myself and experiencing the life-shifting power of her methodology, I used my experiences and knowledge to reframe some of her teachings to help even more people achieve the freedom from stress, anxiety, and overwhelm.

Then coined it as the **Emotional Reset Method**.

And it really works!

Again, the Emotional Reset Method, or ERM, is the act of identifying emotional stumbling blocks from our past (or attachments to stressful inner stories, scenarios, or concepts), and releasing our attachment to those emotions and reconnecting to our true intuition.

It might sound a bit heavy, but it can be fast and easy.

Understanding the Emotional Reset Method

The Emotional Reset Method (ERM) is a 5-step technique to identify, name, and release that feeling or sensation of stress/anxiety/pain/worry that you don't want in your body anymore (so you can move forward with more lightness, freedom, and purpose).

It only takes about 5 minutes, but if you sit, center, and do it with integrity—it can really help you get back to doing what you do—whether that's building a business, taking care of your family, pursuing a relationship, or just enjoying life.

1. Pause. Tune into what you feel.

The first step is to pause. To stop, sit still, and breath deep into your belly. Before you can discover where you're carrying your emotions, you need to ground yourself in your body.

We're often so busy that we spend a lot of our time "out of our bodies". Many mindfulness practices start with the breath, allowing yourself to slow down and bring yourself back "into your body". Think about a tree, when the wind blows, it is the root that lets the wind sway through the limbs without knocking it over. It just takes a minute to breathe deeply, connect your mind and body, and "root" down.

Sit down in a comfy seat and get away from your computer and phone. Place your hands on your thighs, close your eyes, and breathe deeply, starting from your belly (your diaphragm). Slowly count in-and-out for 5 seconds. This will center and ground you. You'll feel more calm and present.

2. Describe it. What do you feel?

Next, ask yourself: What sensation am I feeling? Let go of any self-judgement. There's no need to critique or criticize. The key to this step is to be relaxed and honest with yourself so you can feel into the sensations of your body (and emotions). When you release and let yourself feel, different sensations, emotions, and reactions will come up. Is it anxiety? Is it fear? Maybe you're just... tired? The key here is to just sink in, let yourself feel, and then name that out into the world.

For me, what I was feeling was heavy anxiety and fatigue. A desire to "do it all". That desire to do a million things and trying to fit it all into my chaotic day.

3. Locate it. Where do you feel it?

The third step is to identify where you're feeling it. When I say to locate it... if you're like, what?? Think about this: have you ever been incredibly anxious and worried and you felt a tightening feeling in your stomach or lungs? Have you ever felt like someone laid a giant cinder block on your chest and you could barely breathe? That feeling you perceive is emotion making its presence known physically somewhere. Locate where that place is in your body.

In my case, it was right in the middle of my stomach. That fatigue and anxiety were making itself physically known deep down in my belly. So, I brought my attention to that sensation and location.

4. Give it a visual. Can you describe it as a color?

What's most easy to describe is a color and use it for visualization. You need to be able to visualize this feeling you defined in Step 3. For many, it's easiest to describe it as a color. Just keep that feeling in your mind and say whatever first comes to your head. Is tension a glowing red? Is fear a deep blue? Is anxiety a subtle purple? It will be different for everyone and every sensation, but if you pause and feel it out – you can think of a color that represents this emotion and feeling as you describe that sensation into more thoughts, feelings, words and images. Imagine giving it a voice.

In my case, it was blue. That heavy, radiating feeling in my stomach... was like a deep, fuzzy blue just sitting there. The blue represented the fatigue and anxiety I was feeling over being way too busy and wearing myself thin.

5. Release it. Time to let it go.

Visualize the power of the mind pushing that defined feeling up and out of the body. Once you've named your feeling, located it in your body, and described it, you're ready to let it go—to release it.

Take one more deep breath and then really picture pushing that feeling/color out of your body. Do you feel it sneaking up your chest and out of your head like a mist or cloud? Does it just kind of radiate and seep out of your entire body at once?

Everyone will experience this differently. Feel into it and picture it leaving you. Imagine the emotional block inside you dissolving. Fading out and away. It's time to release.

For my final step, I wanted to release those emotions and find clarity. So I focused and felt a huge release radiate out of my stomach, up through my chest, head and out.

After doing that whole ERM process, I felt such a lightness—a weight lifted— I ended up releasing this ball of stress and fatigue that was inside of me.

With this process, it helped me to remember that I have the power to take charge. To create a plan to take action on what needs to get done and let go of what is not as important as I think it may be.

Sometimes just calling attention to the fact that emotions are affecting us physically can make a big difference.

A friend of mine used ERM to uncover the pain of clenching her jaw on her beautiful, white teeth. As a teenager, every time she'd visit the dentist, they'd peer inside her mouth and exclaim over her fine, straight, white teeth. Until recently, when all that changed.

The last time that friend of mine went to the dentist, it took about two seconds of glancing inside her mouth for the dentist to say: Oh, you're a clincher. The stress my friend had been feeling had manifested itself physically; she was in the middle of a move and job change, and it had wounded her so tightly, she'd expressed the stress by clenching her teeth. Before that point, it had never occurred to her that stress could cause cavities in her teeth and her (otherwise perfectly healthy) gums to wear away.

That's the thing about emotions: Though they seem abstract and intangible, they all make their marks upon us.

Sometimes just calling attention to the fact that emotions are affecting us physically can make a big difference. While the teeth clencher hasn't fully given up her bad habit, knowing that it's caused by stress has made her more aware of her body. When she starts to feel stressed, she pays more attention to her jaw. When she notices she's clenching her teeth, she asks herself, "What am I feeling? And why?" Being aware is the first step in managing your emotions.

I worked with another friend of mine, whose pain was manifesting itself in her chest. I asked her to describe it, and she identified it as the color black. I asked her to share what she associated with it, and she said, "Fear, work, anxiety, hurt, difficulty, lack of time." I then guided her to push that black energy out and away. Five minutes after we'd started, she told me she felt peaceful and serene. The anxiety over her fear of fear of failure at work was calmed, and she was able to use the technique going forward, anytime she began to feel overwhelmed.

The Emotional Reset Method doesn't have to take a long time to change how you're feeling; it's a reset, and it should be used as such.

You may feel silly to say out loud and draw out the emotion that you are feeling, but to allow yourself the opportunity to release its power, is worth a few minutes of feeling silly! And when you are no longer attached to the feeling that is controlling you and preventing you from loving and living, you will find that silliness worth it.

This power lies in all of us. We each have the ability to create the life we dream of, it is just a matter of learning the tools and putting them in your "toolbox." When life gets hard, chaotic, feels out of control, or is just being "life," you can find yourself a place to practice the 5 steps to releasing your emotions that are holding you back.

It may feel challenging to face these emotions and recognize the power they are holding over you. This is the mind. You hold the power within to release them and set yourself free. Depression results from the paralyzed and exhausted state we create for ourselves when we have the internal dialogue related to guilt. Telling yourself that it is "all your fault," and believing it, is so harmful to your spirit, emotions, and physical self. Your emotions will hold you back from accessing your full potential.

Take the story of Jess. She was unemployed for 3 months, just moved to a new city, and needed a job. She started a new job and found a mentor; someone who inspired and motivated her. And from her hard work? She met a new client, a blogger. She realized that this was what she wanted to do. And so she did.

From there she began to integrate her passions into her work; travel, fitness, styling. And as she grew and learned, she continued to put herself out there. She hustled. She worked hard but was still experiencing self-doubt and blockages as she was growing her business.

When the universe provides an opportunity to live your passion, you throw yourself out there and go for it. It's your time to flourish! But there are things that hold us back. For Jess she first thought it was her creativity. It was how to be different. How to reach her customers and show why her boutique and brand is right for them. Thinking outside of the box. But when you dig a little deeper, it is not just about being creative, it is about being unafraid of being creative and trying something new. It is overcoming fear. It is overcoming emotional blocks.

And here is where you can apply the Emotional Reset Method. Like my mentor Dr. Coletta Long said, it is about finding these "frozen blocks of energy," so you can guide into them and release them. Release them to free the space in your heart and creativity. Frozen blocks can be anywhere in the body and can house emotions or negative thoughts. The beautiful thing about this method is that it guides you to these places and gives you the tools to free them.

Jess worked through the Emotional Reset Method with me, first opening her lower energy centers in her stomach, low back, and hips, and then bringing her awareness to her body. The places we hold tension, heaviness or constrictions are often the places we store our frozen energy blocks and emotions. Feeling this tension and then visualizing its presence begins to bring into focus this blockage. For Jess it was the shoulders, and the color was dark and black. Many times we see tension and blockages as dark in color.

With the color and location found, you watch this flow from your body; through the top of your head. As it releases, you give it a voice. You give it thoughts, feelings, words, images. You let them go from your body with its voice. And you can say it out loud as it releases. There is no wrong string of images or words. There may not even be a link you can detect between them, but when it is released, you might feel lighter, clearer or free, like Jess did after she released her fear. Like Jess said, it is like getting a massage for your mind!

Before you can feel dark, tense, weighted down. But after? A sense of calm. A sense that everything will be alright. You have cleared space in your mind, heart, body, and spirit to create all that you know you can do.

Often, when people have experienced a severe illness, they discover at the end how the illness has taught them about themselves; about how to love and respect others (myself included). These feelings are deeper because of their challenge. We learn to appreciate the mess and understand the necessity of it. Sometimes the mess is more important than the beauty. The experience also creates a sense of appreciation for parts of life previously taken for granted.

Each time you face your emotions, understand and release them, you have the opportunity to grow from them and become the person you are meant to be.

SOULWORK 4

For the next three days, identify the strong emotions you feel. Experiment with identifying them in the moment. If you don't have time, reflect on your emotions before going to bed.

Breathe into your Theta rhythm, and practice the Emotional Reset Method. Write down how you now feel.

JOURNAL PROMPT

"They can settle in the subconscious, influencing you without you realizing it. In extreme examples, patients with brain damage can still recall information without knowing that they are doing so. This is because the memory of those things has "hidden" away in the brain in a special place. This means our memories are primitive and multifaceted."

Choose a single, powerful memory that you can recall. It does not have to be a negative memory. Write down as much about this memory that you can define. Try to recall emotions, images, people, words or conversations, etc. When you are done explaining the memory, count how many different and distinct aspects you recalled.

CHAPTER FIVE

GETTING REAL

"Only the truth of who you are, if realized, will set you free."
– Eckhart Tolle

Imagine that there are no coincidences and that we all have a divine appointment to be here together. How would that change your perception of this very moment?

Another way to consider the possibility is that the universe is guiding you and me together to reveal something about our true purpose. We can navigate life a little excited, a little nervous, and a little scared. It is like a game of tag; we are hoping to get chased yet hoping we do not get tagged. Our hearts are bound with anticipation and exertion. When an opportunity comes close, we run in the opposite direction for fear they will "catch" us. As you begin to expand your consciousness, the exhaustion of this game begins to fade. The mess begins to have a bit more beauty to it. You'll begin to notice a more calm, peaceful, centeredness within and see a more accurate meaning of the present.

Life works in a certain way; it has flowing energy, intelligence, and information. This flow guides each instant. When you begin to experience it in your life, you can appreciate the beauty in a single moment. The "little things" will naturally no longer bother you. You are joyful and light. This state opens you to more "coincidences." If you can change your perspective, there are no true "coincidences" or accidents. There is a meaning behind each encounter and moment. As you connect with yourself and the universe, you open the door to see the connections that are possible.

As these moments of divine connection arise, practice recognizing their beauty and ask yourself; "What is here for me at this moment?" and "What is the message I am getting now?" These may seem like challenging questions that will require deep excavation, but the discovery is closer than you think! When you take the time to ask what is there for you, the answer is often already in front of you. The answer can take different forms; the Universe chooses to talk to us in different ways. For some people, it is in the form of creative expressions, like how I express myself through my art, or through a sudden flash/feeling of insight, like you, all of a sudden just know the answer. Sometimes it is a "sign" to why a situation occurred or a connection was formed.

The important part of it is to pay attention. Practice jotting down your coincidences and encounters in a journal or on small sticky notes. Maybe you want to classify these divine appointments as small, medium, large and extra-large or create a special page for each moment so you can refer and add to it throughout time. I love to circle and color/highlight words and phrases that keep appearing. Whatever way you choose to remember and pay attention to your appointments is beautiful.

As you explore more meaning in your life, take time at the end of the day to reflect on the events of your day. Before bed, in your mind's eye, walk through each action you took during the day. Stay objective, an observer. Watch yourself brush your teeth, eat breakfast, get dressed, go to work, lead that meeting, pick up the kids, make dinner, watch TV. Most importantly, reflect on what you said, who you interacted with and how you felt after your time together. Allow yourself to witness and feel the emotions of the day without judging yourself for what you did or how you felt. Maybe you did something that felt embarrassing or maybe something that you are proud of. Be an objective witness without ruminating on these feelings and events, let them pass before you as you move on to see the rest of your day. Consider yourself seeing your day like you would watch a movie; view yourself as the protagonist of the day. You are simply observing the behavior of the main character.

After recalling your day, take note about how it feels to have reflected on your thoughts, behaviors, and actions. Maybe you write this observation down next to the coincidences you have recorded or have another place for these reflections. Whatever it is, make note of you as the main character of your story. Give yourself permission to rest peacefully and let yourself dream.

Use Your Portal of Time Between Consciousness

Being authentically yourself is deeply fulfilling. There is such beauty in uncovering your authenticity that happens through the course of this transformation. Mindfulness, emotional intelligence, a shift in perspective and all the other tools you are learning allow you to take your life to a completely different level. Much of the reflection period illuminates repetition and correlation to images and situations. You'll recognize more opportunities available to you so that when it happens again in the future you are prepared and ready to receive it. It is also a great time to notice the "clues" that are leading your life's direction. Maybe it is a direction you want to let go and change course. The harmful "ruts" in your life are a result of past experiences that you have not resolved yet. Those themes recur in your life until you can open to the experience or let it go. Consider how often you have said, "Why does this keep happening to me?" This is a signal to stop, reflect, uncover the pattern, and resolve it so it stops recurring. Let yourself step out of the victim mindset into the creator mindset and ask yourself the deeper questions. "What is here for me to see." The only "why" in your life that will really serve you is your "why" in your life purpose. When you know your "why" you can let that drive your decisions.

The purpose of this step is to help you shine a light on the patterns and themes operating in your life. You will want to go what I call "back to the basics" and identify what your mind is saying and what your heart is wanting so that you can bring the two into alignment. Some of them are working for you, and you'll celebrate the positive appointments, while others are holding you back from your goals and life of your dreams. Making a conscious choice to change direction will open a new door. Recall your previous Soulwork. What were some of the recurring words, phrases, names, or themes? Write down some of the keywords and concepts here:

_____

_____

_____

Now review your Soulwork reflections and identify more themes. Compare them to your initial reflections. Do you see new themes or more of the same? Record your observations below:

_____

_____

_____

Explore the themes you have identified: are they "coincidences" or patterns you want to keep showing up in your life or things you want to change? Are there things you want a breakthrough in or improve in? What do you see that is holding you back from your goals? Jot down at least 3 areas you want to let go and at least 1 area you want a breakthrough in below:

1. _____
2. _____
3. _____

At this point in your transformation, you have a toolbox full of resources. It's time to take my hand so we can dive even deeper into your inner resources, your beautiful, inner creative spirit.

Imagine that your life is a great "masterpiece." Your life is a work of art. Do you find joy in what you've created? Do you believe in yourself and your inner power to create your life? The beauty in stepping into the mess is seeing the journey as it is and your capacity to cultivate and deepen your potential. This is where the next step is valuable as you begin to write more on these pages.

In the previous chapter, you began reflecting on your experiences and recorded them in writing. During this step, you will dump out all your mental "mess". All the things you are thinking of; your to-do lists, your fears, anxiety burdening your day today. Anything on your mind is to be released onto paper. Just like the exercise above, where you looked back and reflected in your writing, you'll do this with all the mess you are getting out into your journal. As you browse the pages of your journal after dumping into it for a bit, you will notice that little pearls of wisdom will start appearing. And as you continue dumping the mess, and clearing space for yourself, your heart, your creativity, you will start to notice more and more wisdom filling the pages of your book.

The act of journaling is important in bringing your divine appointments and insights to the surface. It helps you become more sensitive to the situations and feelings you have throughout your day and night. This sensitivity to your connection to something larger than you becomes easier when you clear space for a relationship to unfold through your journaling. Let yourself follow the path before you, learning from your present, so you can begin to cultivate the greatest potential lying within.

Be gentle with yourself! Sometimes this is easier said than done! Taking the time to write down your day and thoughts can seem like "another thing to add to your responsibilities." If this is how you are feeling, take a moment and give yourself permission to be compassionate to yourself. If you are a primary caregiver, I want you to say out loud, "I will show compassion; first to myself then to others around me." Repeat as needed until the message becomes a part of you. Life is challenging and complex. Each one of us has obligations, responsibilities, and expectations. With all the whirlwind around you, how can you show compassion to yourself and take care of you?

The time upon waking is a great vortex for your new pathway of communication. There is a moment when your conscious and subconscious are linked. Your inner creative force is guiding you while you sleep, driving your thoughts and your logical mind is beginning to gain awareness. This portal of time is an excellent opportunity to tap into your "dream state" and record your mind's thoughts. Taking 5 minutes when you first wake up to jot down your dreams, thoughts, concerns, desires, and intentions is something I highly recommend. As you continue this practice you will more clearly see how certain people, situations, emotions, and "coincidences" begin to create the answers to the questions you are asking. You are literally writing the answers and guidance to your transformation, creating beauty in the mess.

If you find journaling is a challenge, just keep going. Scribble, draw, repeat the same sentences. Just stay with it. Keep writing whatever comes to you for a set period of time. Setting a timer for 5 minutes allows yourself the chance to dump the mess onto the pages of your journal, and when the timer goes off, you can close your journal and set it aside. What you are writing is building a manual for yourself, one page at a time. If you tried to do this all at once you would most likely freak out! Let it unfold one entry at a time.

When you get these thoughts onto paper, you begin clearing the space for your natural state of a childlike joy. Even when life feels challenging, you'll notice a sense of calm and joy! Connecting to your natural state brings fun back into everything, just by creating space and changing the message!

Megan's journaling journey was like most journeys' start and evolve. Throughout her life, she had always attempted to journal. She would place a notebook by her bed, buy pretty, colorful pens and tell herself that she would fill the pages with wise thoughts and entertaining stories of her day. Of course, she would start strong and then lose steam after a while, finding the pressure of writing all these exciting and inspirational thoughts in her journal was just too much. She would come back to it every now and then, but most of her pages remained blank as her life went on.

When I began working with Megan, she had not written in a journal for a long time. After one of our sessions, I gave her Soulwork to begin journaling when she woke up in the morning. Just like I mentioned earlier about the vortex, I told Megan about the powerful time we can experience when we are between our conscious and subconscious mind and that this is not a time to seek pearls of wisdom, but rather let our mind just write a stream of consciousness for 5 minutes. Keeping a journal with her at all times would help her record the interesting, impactful, funny things happening during the day. Journaling is about freedom; releasing the mess and anything that is clouding your mind.

Megan began trying to journal, without forcing herself or feeling like it was a chore. Some days she would skip writing in her journal while other times she would have a streak for a few days, dumping her thoughts down. Gradually, Megan noticed that her approach to journaling was not personal. She realized that when she wrote in her book she was writing as if someone was going to read her most sincere thoughts. And while I asked her to share some things she had written down to help her on her transformative journey, it was essential that I share with her (and you!) that these pages are for your eyes only. Your writing is for you. Don't worry about spelling, punctuation, and grammar, making it look perfect or complete and keep it in a safe space.

Gaining a solid foundation of an integrated mind and heart through knowledge and personal experience was my pathway to coaching others. As I began working with others in my coaching practice, I more fully experienced the oneness and connection between us all. I continue to feel my heart expanding each and every day as I see how similar we are. It is the stories we tell ourselves that make us appear different.

When feeling an abundance of love around us, most of us immediately constrict to some degree. In the light, there is no constriction, only pure love. Understanding more about spirituality and life, I began to uncover layer after layer of lies I had been telling myself that I thought were true. These stories were from past experiences, teachings and other people and were not in alignment with my own core beliefs. In a conflict between the conscious and the subconscious, the subconscious will win every time.

Because I had lived so many years listening to everyone else, attempting to please others and play the perfect role (whether it be a daughter, sister, significant other, etc), it was a process of understanding my own beliefs, thoughts, and actions. Not owning our worth, knowing our own truth, or looking at how we give away our personal power permeates every aspect of life. Whether it is about relationships, money, love, work, or health, your life will resemble a pendulum. It will swing from the negative pole to the positive pole; one extreme to another, until truth and balance is achieved. We often do not want to see the truth. To some degree, we all feel fear and unworthiness. Awareness is key to transformation. Each and every tool will help you to gain awareness and your journaling process will develop your relationship to your creative force within so that you can continue to evolve your soul.

Imagine scrolling down your social media feed. Most people's thoughts are all over the place, jumping from how long is this going to take to what we need to do next. Sometimes the mind is swimming in negativity, thinking how terrible that girls' outfit looks or how out of shape we feel. Thoughts consume the real estate in our mind and we become numb to the power our thoughts hold. Life is in constant motion and we are constantly creating. If we choose to focus on the past or predict the future, we are not living in the present moment and we are definitely not creating what we really want. This is because we are often not aware of who we are or what we want.

"To know what we really want, we connect the mind and heart."

We cannot attract our dreams and desires when we are not clear on what they are. When we become aware of our own thoughts and stories and the desires that we hold in our hearts, we naturally light the path ahead. Along with my own journey, I discovered that my thoughts consistently repeated to me that I could never "be or do enough". I energetically carried a large amount of fear and unconsciously attracted experiences for the purpose of opening my eyes to the truth. As I slowly uncovered each truth, I made a choice to create new beliefs. These new beliefs reflected the desires in my heart. For example, my heart yearned for more ease in my life. I felt a feeling of hope that I could live my dreams. The thought of my heart stated, "I want to be and do enough." When I was in the state of hope, I would notice the ease and flow in my life. This is the state of a clear, integrated mind and heart.

I felt an ongoing wrestling match in my mind and unmet desires in my heart. As I began to release the illusions in my mind, I saw a new path that does not require years of suffering. I have experienced the range of emotions from deep fear and unimaginable freedom. I have understood what prayer means for me and what God means for me. I believe that we are all on a journey to discover our own truth and live in congruence with the larger universal truths. To experience my personal truth, I learned how to identify what my mind says, what my heart wants and to follow the path of the heart. This path is the path of love.

I believe our sole purpose in life is to love. The key is in loving and trusting yourself. When we focus within rather than everyone and everything outside of us we co-create with life. At times, we all feel like the world is against us when in truth every experience offers an opportunity when we allow ourselves to see it.

I encourage you to use your journal and get creative with it in new ways. Whether it's drawing inspirational images, creating a vision board, or journaling together with friends and family as a way of creating more intimacy in your relationships. One of my closest relationships was with my

Grandmother. I was her caretaker close to the end of her life and one of our activities was completing a journal of her life. I had purchased it at a local Christian store as a holiday gift without knowing the power it would have. This journal was like a history book, recalling every aspect of her life from birth to present. At the age of 93, her arthritis prevented her from writing easily so we would go through the journal together and I'd write down her answers. It was so beautiful to hear her recalling memories and share the good, bad, happy and sad times. I could feel her joy, love, frustration, anger, peace and every other emotion that surfaced throughout the adventure. Although I didn't realize it at the time, once she passed, I connected the dots and similar to my studies on near-death experiences and experiencing what was called a life review, I realized that the journaling had prepared her to face her own self. She had so much courage through her last few days that I knew in my heart she was ready. I let her know that it was ok. I gave her permission to go when she was ready and to this day it was one of the hardest things I have ever done. It was also one of the most loving things I've done and I could feel the love carrying me through it. She knew how difficult my Father's death had been for me and although she never expressed it, I knew how hard it was for her. For the first time, I was able to see the beauty in experiencing her death. I knew she would feel so much love and peace and would always be with me, just in a different way.

The thoughts of the mind and the heart are very subtle, yet both contain the power to create in every moment.

Starting your journaling journey with just five minutes a day in the morning will offer you significant transformation.

SOULWORK 5

For the next three to four days, surround yourself with a state of direction. Through your exercises in this chapter, certain themes will arise, such as disappointment in people and situations, or anger when "things don't go your way." What is it about the scenarios you wish to transform? Are you ready to release your expectations? Do you want to approach a situation with love and light instead of anger and frustration?

Write down a few words on three to four sticky notes and place them somewhere you'll see them often, such as the microwave, your computer, on your nightstand, or in your car. Check in with yourself and your transformation. Write down your reflections in your journal.

JOURNAL PROMPT

"Check in with yourself and your transformation."

Write down your reflections of your transformation in your journal. Take an honest and non-judgmental look at how you are working through your transformation and record it here. Is there anything that you feel or that stands out to you regarding your reflections?

PART TWO

Clarity in Your Connection

CHAPTER SIX

LOVE YOUR PERSONAL MESS

"We can see the Divine in each speck of dust, but that does not stop us from wiping it away with a wet sponge. The Divine does not disappear; it is transformed into the clean surface."
– Paulo Coelho

Congratulations! You've made it through what I call the "basics." Any time you feel like you want to reset your mind and tune into your heart, you can go do so by going back to the basics. With practice, it becomes easier and easier to reconnect. The "new" and beautiful world you are embarking on is unknown and possibly outside of your comfort zone, yet it is full of love, joy, and light. That is not to say that you will not experience heartache, pain, and grief. Our life experiences are the greatest gift when we can understand where our heart lies and how to navigate our emotions. It is like you are returning to a childlike state of bliss, where the scraped knee hurts for a moment, but it doesn't stop you from getting back on your bike and shifting your focus back on to the feeling of the wind on your face as you race down the hill.

This transformation is a process of up's and down's. You will soar, moving along with the pace of the life, and then stumble and fall. When you fall, you choose to get back up, brush off the dirt, bandage the wounds, and move on again. In time we see how life is about the journey rather than the end result. It's about the times we rise and fall. You transform during those moments. Bring your awareness to your personal journey and let go of how you "think" it is supposed to un-fold. Let go of the things that you no longer need, and make space to welcome in the things that you need. As you cultivate your intuition and live from a new perspective, you will learn more about what works for you and what doesn't. And the more you learn, the more aware you become. It is a beautiful cycle, beautiful and messy. Embracing the contrast of the beauty and the mess will show you how to love your personal mess!

Life works in a certain way; it has flowing energy, intelli-gence, and information. This flow guides each instant. When The next time you feel yourself spiraling into the chaos, take a few minutes or even seconds and step back. Ask yourself the following questions:

What can I learn from this experience?
What is here for me?
In the future, what would I do differently?

If you've hit bottom and go back to the basics, notice what is helping you up. It can be a new thought pattern, someone or something, but see if you can put your finger on what helped you up from the ground. Was it something internal or external? The more that you rely on your new tools and cultivate your intuition, the more power you create. What you observe in these situations can provide you with powerful tools that you can store in your toolbox.

Your personal transformation has already begun. You're beginning to tap into who you really are. Think about all the time you have dedicated to uncovering your true self. Remember the emotions you have already released and the reflections of how you want to direct your life. Recall the sticky notes you wrote and stuck all over the place.

What was the most transformational sticky note you wrote? What did it say? Write it out again below:

_____

_____

_____

Now read back through your journal and your thoughts about this direction. How do you feel? What was harder than you expected? What was easier? When you followed the direction you set forth for yourself, did you feel joy, release, happiness, a connection to something greater? Reread your reflections and summarize how you felt and what was happening that allowed you to follow your intention:

1. _____

2. _____

3. _____

Now shift your focus; what threads underline the times when you felt challenged to follow your new direction? Is there anything that stands out to you? Is there a recurring pattern? Reread your reflections, and take the time to identify at least 3 significant discoveries that prevented you from following your desire.

1. _____

2. _____

3. _____

We are learning more and more how we hold the power to change our own state of mind. We begin by changing our belief in ourselves so that we can release the obstacles and begin to identify with new resources. I learned through my mentor Dr. Coletta Long, beliefs cause our behavior to rise to meet our expectations. The belief of tapping into our subconscious, pulling out more potential, and rising above the fear that limits is how Dr. Long has trained me to help people create lasting change. Our new behavior goes into action and through trial and success is ready to move to a higher level—all based on our beliefs.

Imagine the conscious mind as a window through which you look outward and perceive the fruits of your subconscious mind. The subconscious also has access to all of the creative energy and wisdom of the universe and draws upon that energy when the energies of fear are not dominating your conscious mind. This means that your joy, vitality, and accomplishment do not come from the outside as the result of events that "happen to you"; they manifest from the inner processes of the subconscious mind that result from your beliefs.

The subconscious can be drawing upon information or energy that may be the source of our problems. Yet, although we often let false beliefs blur that great vision, we do have the power to let go of these beliefs and clarify our vision. This is when we can feel the vision in our heart and let the feeling guide us toward the desire. Knowing the universal laws and the way the mind works can help integrate a solid understanding. My mentor, Dr. Long developed "The 50 Principles of the Universe" with five other pioneers in the field of regression. The document states, "The universe is perfectly balanced by moral and natural laws which are regulatory vibrations to maintain order. When you work within the laws you can be assured of the eventual positive outcome. When the laws are transgressed you can be assured of suffering, the only purpose of which is to teach a better way." I have recorded the 50 Principles of the Universe and you can download the MP3 on my website at http://www.robinemmerich.com/50. Listen daily to train your mind and receive radical transformation.

We will be diving into a few of my favorites for more understanding.

The Law of Growth is one of the easiest laws to understand.

All of life is in a constant state of growth. Or another way to say this is that everything is always transforming, even you! Your growth has been determined by the seeds you have planted in the past, and your future transformation will depend on what you choose to plant now. If you have decided you want to grow in love, harmony, peace, and happiness, you need to plant those seeds now so you can grow into those states of being.

In short, through seeking wisdom and living in the expression of love, we naturally find harmony and balance. It is when we are living life full out in love and harmony that we no longer carry the karma that is pulling us towards experiences that we chose to help us learn in the school of life. We are here to evolve our souls and we are the only ones that are in control of the choices we make and actions we take.

A friend of mine arrived one day torn over her current intimate relationship. As she opened up about the relationship, she stated that she was afraid of staying in the relationship in case things didn't work out. In truth, she had been on a beautiful path of personal growth and for the first time in her life, she had attracted a man that was willing to commit to her, willing to learn and grow, and wanted to learn to communicate together. I suggested that we start with the thoughts in her mind, which she identified as "I am afraid of making a mistake." Once she said it out loud, she followed with, "I don't deserve a relationship." These thoughts were keeping her stuck and holding her back from having the relationship she wanted.

Through my Emotional Reset Method, we released the energy of fear and received clarity on her truth. Receiving what she had wanted for so long brought up another layer of fear. To some level, we are all afraid of not being loved and accepted. Until we uncover the thought pattern or doubt, we cannot work with the fear. Creating the awareness, uncovering the truth and choosing to accept it would allow her to move forward. Her heart desired to be in a healthy relationship, and raise a child from that place. She had grown up in a dysfunctional family and did not want to repeat the same patterns. She was divinely guided to a man that was into personal growth, desired a healthy family and wanted children as well. Knowing that sometimes our biggest fear is standing in our own power, I asked her, "What would it be like for you to stand fully in your power and trust yourself enough to give the relationship a chance?"

What is true is that there are no guarantees, but how would it feel to not take the risk? She immediately knew that it was time to commit to her own heart and step fully into the relationship. When we commit to our own hearts to make the choices that are in our highest good, we hold the power to take control of our lives.

Through this process, one of the common challenges people face is, "I don't know what I want yet." It is completely normal. Our purpose is to discover our desires and have fun in the process! Once we start, we begin to learn more about what we want. Sometimes it is necessary to experience the contrast of what we don't want so that we can see what we do want. Life constantly provides the contrast to guide us in the journey. When we can see what we don't want, we can turn it around and discover what we do want.

As the heart awakens, new desires often emerge. Clarity on what we desire and why creates conscious change. To change the belief system may require a loss of support in our present environment. Even though it is not working, we may fear that a replacement might give us less. The fear leads us to cling to what we already have because we haven't experienced the support within ourselves. Connecting with our own inner strength and power allows us to create authentic change.

Without growth and challenges, we often experience discontent and rarely growth without discomfort. As frustration rises, we are receiving a signal to look at what is ready to be set free or a new direction ahead. We always know what is best for ourselves. Awareness is the key to choosing happiness and success. How can you use the law of growth to create the change that you want to see in your life?

Now let's look at the Law Of Harmony.

You're meant to live a balanced life. You can learn the balance through the understanding of cause and effect. Imagine a placid lake. It is still and calm, until something disturbs it, like a rock being tossed into it. The water ripples and splashes in all directions, until it slowly finds its way back to harmony after the disturbance is gone. This is the same in your life. When you remove the disturbances, your life may continue to splash around a little bit until it settles back into balance.

This is the law that helped me understand that there are truly no mistakes. We have unlimited opportunities to experience the ripples of life that will eventually result in harmony.

Think of it this way, the "right" thought of action has one course. The "wrong" has an infinite number of possibilities. When something "wrong" happens, it sets off a series of reactions inside you and around you. You are forced to explore a path that you did not look down before or did not want to follow on your own. It allows for you to make connections that are new and innovative to your "old, right" way of life. In the fabric of our lives, most of our defining moments are results of something that went "wrong." And while these moments can often be scary, hurtful, and sorrowful, they are what led you further down to discovering the great things in your life, like love, support, and happiness.

My client Megan was in a long-term relationship and wanted to learn how to improve it. She felt that she and her partner were growing apart and wanted to understand if it was in her highest good to stay in the relationship. I walked her through the methodology shared in the previous chapters and we uncovered the cause: her core thought pattern of taking on responsibility for others and ignoring her own truth/ intuition, the effect unfolded. As she began to understand more of who she was and what her heart wanted, she discovered that her partner had been cheating on her for the past ten years. It was something she knew earlier in the relationship and believed it would never happen again. She ignored her intuition to leave the relationship thinking that the doubt she felt around her relationship was something she needed to change. This was her defining moment, which was heartbreaking and confusing almost ten years later. Yet it led her to freedom to let go of a relationship that was no longer in balance and create a new path. She is now full of love, creativity, self-trust and confidence to follow the Light in her heart. With an open mind and understanding of the laws of the universe, she is continuing to follow her heart with a knowing that life experiences will find their way back to harmony.

The Law Of Harmony is directly influenced by the Law of Karma. This is the cause and effect part of it. Your actions have consequences, and the experience of your consequences is karma. Whatever you choose to do, there is a consequence. And remember, your actions are a result of your beliefs. So your beliefs determine your actions, which end in a related result. Your motivations and intentions behind your actions are powerful sources of Karma. When you develop a belief that is clear and aligned with your heart, and not from a place of fear, your actions are more harmonious. When you are out of harmony, you can learn an important lesson, in addition to learning more about the Law of Karma.

When you began your journey, you were probably curious about how to find the best "version" of yourself. You wanted to know more about who you truly are and what your purpose is. This curiosity develops your Karma. Each time you reflect on your transformation and find an area that you do not have the "answers" for, you open the door for Karma. Karma wants you to find the answers, so it reveals a situation in order for you to discover the truth. When you identify a gap in your understanding, wait for the experience that will develop your awareness and fill that opening.

As Megan discovered, her partner was there to show her that she was ready to start listening to her intuition and follow her heart.

I believe The Law Of Wisdom is the most motivational in our daily lives.

It is basically helping us understand that we have the choice to see the wisdom in a situation and clear our Karma. I'll say it again.... YOU have the choice to see the wisdom in a situation and release your own Karma. When we can choose to see the truth, we set ourselves free.

When Karma presents you with a lesson, you have the choice to learn from it or ignore it. Most people find it easier to ignore the lessons of life, but if you face each lesson and learn from it, you open the opportunity to gain insight and experience the law of wisdom. Wisdom clears your Karma. Pain and suffering are powerful teachers, but they are not the only ones.

The insight you have gained throughout the course of this book has helped you clear your Karma. Part of the process is to show you the lessons of your life and also release the pain and negativity that can come with those lessons. When you allow yourself to let go of the suffering, you can wisely learn your lesson through love and understanding. This wisdom allows you to take a step back and recognize that you are learning a lesson from your past beliefs and actions, and now you can decide to learn from it and move forward. This ability is a potent step in your transformation.

The Law Of Unconditional Love

The expression of unconditional love will eventually result in harmony. Unconditional love is not romantic love it's the acceptance of others as they are without judgment or expectation. It's the total acceptance of others, without attempting to change them except by your own positive example. The law of unconditional love says, if you go out of your way to express unconditional love, you automatically rise above fear, and as you transcend your fears you automatically open to the expression of unconditional love.

Loving yourself and others give you the boost necessary to move away from fear and towards harmony. And the beautiful thing about unconditional love? The more you give, the more you get in return! And there is no limit! This is why you can love your own mess, and others, and still have more. When you do something with love, without judgment or expectation of anything in return, you carve the river of love deeper and wider.

The Law Of Commitment

Your commitment to harmony and truth is like a magnet that pulls your desires to you. It draws what you want and need to you, putting the puzzle pieces into place. The secret? Be clear. Set your intention on where you want to go. This does not necessarily mean you need to define your next romantic partner by name or height, but rather that you are clear you want to find a compatible and loving partner or a supportive group of friends.

When you become clear on your intent making a decision and obligating yourself to a task or a belief everything begins to fall into place if your direction is in harmony with the universe as it relates with your purpose. Once you are devoted to your purpose, things begin to happen almost magically as if you were a magnet drawing into your experience that which is needed for a manifestation. The key to this ultimate power is to have no indecisiveness at all and the greater the emotional desire the more power you will feel.

Prior to your understanding of this Universal law, you have worked through several exercises and Soulwork related to helping you define your clear intentions. Commitment to this desire for truth and being steadfast protects your resolve when life inevitably sends waves crashing against your soul. When you are firm in your convictions, the waves will break and scatter instead of dragging you back into despair.

The Law Of Self-Worth is your power.

It is related to your beliefs as well, but it is about your be-lief in your self-worth. You bring to you what you feel you are worthy of gaining. Fear typically holds you back from bringing in what you really want. When you strip fear away, more and more opportunity presents itself. As opportunity flows in, you become more confident, are open to more risks, establish connections with people, and are a formidable ex-ample of unconditional love. Your self-worth is connected to your self-esteem. The more you love yourself the happier you will become.

To help identify your self-worth, look closely into a mir-ror. Study your facial features. Look for features you find strong, powerful, unique, and beautiful. This could be a strong jaw or intelligent eyes. Or it could be your full eyebrows or grey hair. Whatever you see, do not negatively judge your features. Do not allow yourself to fall into thinking about what you "should" look like. The purpose is to find even something small that is connected to your being. Age spots and wrinkles show the years earned, not a weakness. Full lips or cheeks show health and vitality.

This reflection of your face is a seat of self-power and self-worth. And that is only your face! Imagine if you took a step back and observed your whole body and then dove into your soul. Think about how boundless your power is! Take this realization, and any time something does not vibe with this truth, release it back out. It does not serve your greater pur-pose.

Get Clear, Not Fear

As you move along in your personal journey, schedule time for yourself to sit down and reflect on all the things you've explored during the course of this book. All the challenging emotions you've released and seen in a new light, all the things you want to let go, and the beauty you want to create. When you uncover what is true for you, the light within will continue to grow and direct you in your purpose.

Self-trust and commitment to your own self are what will create lasting transformation. Experiencing your truth; that you already are love and joy will catapult your transformation and help you believe in you. In time, you'll begin to see more and more how the "bad" and "mistaken" situations were placed in your path to show you something and evolve your soul. Just as planting a seed for a flower to grow means you must nurture it before you see the blossom, you, too, must plant your seed of intention, nurture it with love, compassion, and acceptance, and enjoy the process as you watch your life blossom.

And when your blossom is in full bloom, standing tall and bright, facing the sun, you can see the beauty you've been nurturing all along.

PERSONAL SOULWORK 1

From this section and into the next chapters, you are moving beyond releasing your emotions and are getting to the "heart" of your present day so that you can live your purpose.

You'll begin on the first day with a 5-minute meditation. Follow the guided script provided below or find your own way into your Theta rhythm. Once you are in your meditative state, and if you are using the script below, reach down and pick up the 4 stones. The three white stones represent each of the things you want to gain. The single black stone is one thing you want to release. As you pick up the first stone, tell yourself what it represents and throw it into the river. Do this with all 4 stones. If you are in your own meditative state, bring these 4 things; 3 things you desire, and 1 you wish to release, to your mind's eye. Form a thought and your attention around each one and then release them into the Universe. You are no longer attached to them. When you are done, bring yourself out of your meditation. When you come out of your meditation, write down the 3 things you desire and the 1 you released.

On the second day, grab a piece of poster board and a marker. On one side write the one thing you want to release, and on the other write the 3 things you want to bring in. Keep it simple and clean. As you record them on this poster, take time to reflect on what you desire and do not need any longer.

On the third day, seek out images and other words to place around the 3 things you want. Look in magazines or online to find inspiration to put all around what you want to bring into your life. Print, cut out, and glue onto your poster, only on the side written with what you want. Leave the side with what you want to release plain. Focus all your energy on this positive task; these are the seeds you are planting and nurturing.

On the fourth day, place your poster in a spot where you will see it often. The bathroom or side of your bed is a great location. Adjust the location if you need to so you get the maximum opportunity for seeing your messaging. Just display the side with the images you want to bring into your life.

On the fifth day, write your 3 things onto a sticky note and place them in locations you will see them. Write all 3 on one sticky note, but make sure you write out multiple sticky notes to place all around. Continue to move or create more sticky notes as you need them over the next few days.

On the seventh day, bring yourself back into a meditative state, again, following the guided meditation below or coming into your own. Return to the place you cast your desires into the Universe, and take a moment to silently check in. See if you recognize a sign from the Universe that guided you this week. Did something unfold that was aligned with your new goals or assisted you in letting go of the one thing you gave back that you no longer needed? Take this time to look at the movement and growth you are already creating, even if it is small!

Remember, growth occurs well before your eye can see it. Again, think of planting a little seed in a large flower bed. You place it under the Earth and give it food and water, but you have no idea if there is anything happening. While you may not see it on the surface, there is a flourishing of life and growth occurring. The seed is splitting open, the roots are reaching far into the ground, and the sprout is pushing up towards the surface. If you don't see your own growth at this point, that is ok. This just means your roots are drawing down and your seed is splitting open. Continue to nourish your desires and keep an eye on your garden. One day you will see the little mound of earth and your sprout pushing through, and then you will see it shoot for the sky and take shape. If today your "sprout" is not visible in your meditation, just remember this and trust in the process. You are transforming!

GUIDED MEDITATION SCRIPT

Use this guide to help you reach into your Theta rhythm if you feel it will help you in your journey:

Begin by finding a comfortable position. Close your eyes if that feels good to you, or find a place to softly gaze. As you settle in, bring your breath to your stomach. Exhale. Breathe into your hips. Exhale. And finally, breathe into your lower back. Exhale.

Imagine yourself walking along a forest riverbank. The sun is warm above you. The soft wind is cooling and you listen as it ruffles the leaves of the trees around you. Take a moment to look at the trees. See their bark and stems. Look up into their branches and then all the way down to its roots disappearing in the ground. Follow the direction of the roots diving into the earth and follow along with the moss and lush foliage on the ground that leads to the bank of the river you are standing next to. Notice how thick and vibrant the ground looks along the side of the river.

Now, look into the river. Watch the water as it moves over the stones. Listen to the sound of it rushing along. Look down by your feet and notice there are river stones near where you are standing. Among the stones are 3 pure white rocks and 1 dark black one. Reach down and feel the 4 stones in your hands. Pick them up and feel their weight as you hold each one. Each white stone, you know, represents a desire you have for your life. Something you want to have a breakthrough in. Maybe it is love or friendship. Maybe it is family, health, or joy. Take a moment to discover the desire each white stone represents in your life. Now bring your attention to the single black rock in your hands. This rock is heavier than the others and it is something you need to release from your life. Maybe this is an emotion you are having a hard time releasing, or a person you need to let go, or a situation you do not want to occur. Whatever it is, the rock holds its meaning.

You reach into your pocket and take out a pen. You then write your desires on the 4 rocks, making it clear what you want and do not want any longer. As you finish writing, you place the pen back in your pocket and take the first, black rock. You pick it up and hurl it into the river. You then do the same for each of the white rocks. Hurling each, one at a time, into the rushing river. Watch as each splash into the river and the ripples begin to fade as the water rushes on. As you watch each one fade into the river, know that challenging situations and people come into your life to help you grow and transform. Be in gratitude for the lessons but know that they no longer serve you. Now that you have planted your desires in the river you are ready for the Universe to guide them back to you in the forms that you need.

You are ready to leave the riverbank, and as you walk away you feel taller. There are new possibilities all around you. You follow a well-worn tree-lined path, a path that represents your personal transformative journey. As you walk you see all the things you want to bring into your life. Everything you desire to be happy, in harmony, and balanced stands along the path as you walk along. As you near the end of the path there is a golden door. You feel the glow on your skin and the love it is radiating. As you approach closer to the door you realize there are other travelers headed to the door near you. At first, you do not see their faces, but as you get nearer and nearer you begin to recognize the people who are on this journey with you.

You begin to walk beside some of these other travelers, feeling light and peaceful. You know that the door will open. You know that on the other side is the transformation you desire. You know that when you walk through that door you will never be the same.

Allow yourself to stand on the other side of the door, while you bring yourself back to consciousness, slowly bringing movement back into your body, and when you are ready, open your eyes. If you feel that you need to, write down how you are feeling, how your heart is feeling, and the thoughts that are bubbling inside you. Know that at any point you can bring yourself back to this place to see your desires and your journey towards your golden door of transformation.

JOURNAL PROMPT

"When Karma presents you with a lesson, you have the choice to learn from it or ignore it. Most people find it easier to ignore the lessons of life, but if you face each lesson and learn from it, you open the opportunity to gain insight and experience the law of wisdom. Wisdom clears your Karma. Pain and suffering are powerful teachers, but they are not the only ones."

Record a time you learned a valuable lesson but did not have to suffer to learn it. Identify what it was that taught you the lesson. Think about other times this same teacher appeared to you. Did you learn a lesson in that situation, too?

CHAPTER SEVEN

TURN THE LIGHT ON

"And the day came when the risk to remain tight in a bud was more painful than the risk it took to blossom."
– Anais Nin

There is an ebb and flow to life and at times, you'll come to a place in your life that feels like a crossroads. You'll be in a transition and may feel confused about where to go next. It is an uncomfortable state. This point in your transformation illuminates the direction you had once been traveling and the stagnation ahead, while the other paths offer an unknown transformation. Here you stand, presented with the opportunity to transform into your true self or continue to stay in your comfortable and familiar façade.

Change is challenging and messy. When you remove the false sense of self and expose your true desires, you open yourself to the risk of change. As a Western society, we analyze situations like this in a "risk-reward" scenario. Is the risk associated with change less than the risk associated with staying on the current course? The reality is, yes, the risk of changing into who you are meant to be, or rather rediscovering who you truly are, is far less risky than continuing to deny the power inside of you.

Self-doubt and insecurity can take hold of you and these "voices" can become so loud that it is hard to think of anything else. This makes this crossroads challenging to navigate openly. Overcoming the negative inspirations will allow you to move forward.

A personal friend of mine, a beautiful, successful, young woman, confided in me that she was struggling with her confidence. Most people would look at her and feel that she had no reason to lack confidence, yet she struggled with what many women struggle with; self-judgment and doubt in her ability. Before our discussion, she had been socializing more because of her new sales position. She was spending more time around other successful and beautiful people, and the voices in her head began to make her feel insecure about herself. When the night would grow quiet, she began to feel like an "imposter" and "not good enough."

If my friend had allowed these voices to grow any stronger, she would have risked them taking a hold of her life and spiraling her life downwards. The power of these negative, internal voices can drive what you do or do not do, how to live or do not live your life, and tell you that you are not good enough for anything. If you give in to these voices now, you'll believe that you are not powerful enough to stand next to other successful people, or bond with a new friend, or take the risk of unveiling your true self.

The person you are meant to be can be shut out by these voices, but you have the ability to not listen to them. Every time a thought appears that is negative, it is important to turn it from being critical to positive. For example, "I'm not good enough" is rephrased as "I am enough!" Taking the following week to practice her new mantra allowed her to break through her self-criticism and recognize her true strength and ability. I knew she was more than capable and now she knows it too!

We connect ourselves to people, places, and things rather than connecting with our true self inside. There is an inner peace waiting for you, but you must be willing to accept the truth of your own self. You have the power to accept or reject your own self. As you reflect on your internal dialogue, you will identify thought patterns that no longer serve you. Rejecting these thoughts creates a space for new inspiration to be born. When you connect with your true and highest self, you begin to know the still and unshakable self. Once you accept your true self there is no turning back to the old path.

My life was once filled with a rigid, self-imposed structure, a host of "should's" I adhered to daily, and a fruitless pursuit of perfection. I had already begun growing in my own awareness but I found new growth when I forced myself into situations that kept me present and alive in the moment. When curiosity was the leader, instead of judgment and negativity, the weight of my own thoughts disappeared. The heaviness that lived in my mind was relieved. Instead, I was living through the joy and freedom in my heart. I was excited for the next moment with anticipation that the next open door held, a part of me that I had not experienced before. The experiences that brought me to this state will forever be a part of my life and heart.

My experiences came from following my intuition. I chose to reframe the negative voices in my mind and follow my instinct. If I had listened to the voices, I would have justified it saying I was being practical and focused, but I knew I could not allow the voices in my head to limit me. If you limit yourself by listening to these voices, you limit your life's opportunities as well!

In every moment, we have the opportunity to co-create with the Universe. When we ignore what is on our heart, we ignore the possibilities that can manifest through our heartfelt desires.

This next step in your personal transformation is to listen to your internal dialogue, identify the negative voices that are limiting your potential, and flip the switch to a positive message.

The "How To" Flip the Negative Voices

There is a trick to flipping the switch and overcoming the negativity: listen for the voice, identify it, and consciously change it to a positive message. To first identify the voice, you need to pay attention to your internal dialogue that is always negative and constantly holds you back. These voices are what set your limits and drag you backward. Take a moment over the next few days and identify the negative voices bouncing around in your head. Write down at least three negative messages in your head here:

1. _____
2. _____
3. _____

Now that you have the awareness of these voices holding you back, take each phrase you wrote down above and change it into a positive message.

As you increase your awareness of these negative influences in your life, the ones that hold you back from being your authentic self, you can change the internal dialogue to support your true self rather than keep it from being who you are.

There are a few keys to help you continue bringing awareness to your voices and to your true self:

- **Let go of who you think you are "supposed to" be or "should" be.**
- **Begin to look within (who you are on the inside.)**
- **Recognize that letting go of who you think you "should be" opens the door for growth and transformation.**
- **Identify the parts of yourself that stay with you no matter what changes are happening around you.**

You have planted the seed for your personal transformation in the previous chapter, and now it is time to feed that little, budding seed love and Light, and remove any negative and destructive influences. Removing these negative voices and replacing them with soul-nourishing affirmations is what will turn your little seed into a blossoming flower. To start, you just need to allow change to be more beneficial than staying stuck on your current course.

Remember to focus on your heart space. As you begin to discern these new insights just feel your heart and take a breath into it. All of the answers are within.

When we focus on the desires of the heart, we draw the energy of the heart into our physical experience, consciously creating our heart's desires. Life just feels good when we are living from our heart. This is because we are creating what we most want rather than living from our conscious mind—limited in what is truly possible, often creating everything that we don't want. In a conflict between the conscious and the subconscious, the subconscious will win every time. It is the stories we tell ourselves that make life complicated. As we learn to let go of the stories and connect the mind and heart, beautiful transformations unfold.

We cannot attract our dreams and desires when we are not clear on what they are. To know what we really want, we must get clear on what our mind is thinking and what our heart is wanting. When we become aware of our own thoughts and stories and the desires that we hold in our hearts, we naturally light the path ahead. Envision waking up in the dark in a new environment. Without knowing which direction to turn, you find yourself stumbling. Finding a tiny night light next to your bed, it radiates just enough light to see a path ahead. The path is there, yet the action is still required to move from the dark into the light. The action is to listen to the light in your heart and follow your own inner GPS.

To move beyond the mess and into clarity.

After working with thousands of clients, I discovered a theme in core thought patterns. One of the three most common is "I am not worthy of love." This thought pattern will feel an ongoing wrestling match in our minds and unmet desires in our hearts until we learn how to access the desires of our hearts. To begin listening to the thoughts in the heart, it is helpful to keep a running list of the thoughts in the mind that feel negative and restricting as described above. Then take that list to uncover the thoughts in the heart. The thoughts of the heart will feel positive and hopeful. As you practice differentiating the thoughts of your heart, pay close attention to those thoughts. In noticing those thoughts, I was able to see how the thoughts of my heart contrasted with my mind's thoughts. Eventually, I realized that I had to make a choice: Do I choose to follow my mind or my heart?

In my experience, the process was very slow in the beginning. I was not used to the feeling and had been so disconnected from myself for so long, I felt a discomfort and lack of trust in my ability to discern the truth. Often about half of my clients struggle with tuning into their heart and the other half quickly tune in and take off. We are all unique and on different paths. For many, it can literally feel like learning to walk again. You may find your heart wanting to run toward your dreams, while your mind wants to make every excuse of why your dreams are out of reach. Becoming aware will allow you to question the thoughts in your mind and check in with your heart. Pay close attention to how each thought feels. This path is the path of the heart. It begins with first identifying the voice of the mind and the voice of the heart.

As a society, we are so focused on work and achievement that when we slow down to understand why we do the things we do, we feel a sense of discomfort. It takes practice to own who we are, our value, our worth, our truth. It's important to know that you are not alone. As children, we know that we are loving, creative forces and as we grow older, the voices of other people begin to slowly drown our own inner voice.

What do you really want?

Ashley, a corporate professional in her late 20s, scheduled a package of twelve coaching sessions with me looking to better understand why she felt as though she was currently living a life that she felt she would have never chosen for herself. In the seventh grade, she dreamt of creating her own makeup line inspired by Estée Lauder, falling in love, and starting a family. Looking at her life now, Ashley had let go of starting her own company and was in a job that felt unfitting and overwhelming, only attracted the men she didn't want and felt embarrassed that her friends were the only ones having children. She had graduated from college six years prior, and despite feeling as though her life was planned out, she felt unprepared for what life had presented after college. Although she did her best to have a positive attitude and feel happy, she was continually telling herself that in time, life would be better than she could imagine. Deep down though, she felt that she was on a hamster wheel that she could not get off.

In her first session, we began by exploring the thoughts in her mind. She said, "I've wasted so much time. There must be something wrong with me to feel this upset and pathetic. When I hear myself, I think, Wow, you are being ridiculous." Her conscious mind was in immediate judgment. She continued with the next thought, Being the oldest, my parents went through everything first with me. This was her rational, logical mind trying to make sense of why she was living a life she would not have picked. And then the realization hit her, "When something gets hard, I want to run and give up. Always. Even as a child."

Her heart was ready to take an honest look at her soul journey and at the thoughts repeating in her mind that were holding her back from the desires in her heart. She stated, "I want to be someone who is happy and loves life." Although she did not yet consciously understand the difference between the thought of her mind telling her she was wasting time and the thought of her heart telling her she wanted to love life, she was now ready with an openness that she did not have in the beginning.

As I guided her to identify the core thought pattern in her mind, she discovered her truth, "I can't trust myself." She then continued, "When I make a decision, it always seems to be the wrong one." This thought pattern was affecting every area of her life. In truth, there is no right or wrong, and this can be a tough concept for many people to grasp. As she acknowledged the thought pattern, she immediately realized that she had held herself stuck for all these years. Accepting her personal truth offered her an opportunity to wake up.

She watched herself as if she was looking down on that past experience and realized that while her mind wanted to beat herself up, her heart wanted to love life. In those moments she granted herself permission to see the truth—she was ready to choose the voice of her heart, and stated, "I want to trust myself." With her new awareness and authoritative conviction, she said, "I already feel like I can breathe a little bit. Deep down I do know the right decision."

Ashley's experience was an incredibly beautiful illustration of life and the power that we hold. We all have a choice, but our task lies in acquiring the ability to attune ourselves to the source of all truth, all knowledge, wisdom, and love. We can then make an empowering choice that moves us toward what we most desire. With this new understanding, she stated, "My decisions will lead me to where I need to be." Ashley formed a new belief for herself based on the truth of her heart. The journey of recognizing her own truth allowed her to organically reprogram her mind with a new, positive thought pattern and allowed her to begin to feel the expansiveness of the light in her heart. And yes, Ashley is now married to an amazing man with a brand-new little girl.

Focusing on what feels good, draws more of it to us. What is most important is carving out space in our day to take time to listen, develop the skill of listening, and gain the inner strength to follow our own guidance. In the toolbox below, you will find the steps to begin identifying what your mind is thinking and what your heart really wants. I highly encourage you to find a quiet spot in nature or somewhere that feels open to you. As you get to know the thoughts of your mind and heart, do your best to hold a loving, non-judgmental space for yourself. You may find that your mind can be really harsh and critical. If it feels too overwhelming, reach out to a trusted mentor or friend for help. It takes time to unravel the thought patterns that have built up over the course of our lives and get clear on what is really true. It's easiest to start small, such as deciding what to eat for example, rather than something significant like ending a relationship. The thoughts of the mind and heart will become more clear in time and trust will begin to build.

Experiment with what feels right for you. We are all unique. If you are like me, you may start with identifying the voices in your mind before attempting to tune in to the voices in your heart. Recording your thoughts in a small notepad, journal, or in your phone will help reveal what your mind is repeating over and over.

It takes time to journey into the heart.

In essence, we are building the muscles of the mind and heart so that we can build an inner strength and choose a new path. Starting with just five minutes a day in the morning or late afternoon will offer significant awareness and open up space for transformation.

PERSONAL SOULWORK 2

The thoughts of the mind and the heart are very subtle, yet both contain the power to create in every moment. To begin connecting your mind and heart try the following:

1. Notice the thoughts in your day-to-day life that feel critical and constricting. What is the exact voice that is playing over and over in your mind?
2. Contrast this voice with the more hopeful and expansive voice of your heart. Dig deep into your heart. What do you most want to feel or experience?
3. Choose your path. Make a new choice: Are you willing to commit to the truth in your heart? How does it feel to believe that you can fulfill your heart's desire?

As you learn more and discover more, I want you to ask yourself: what is one commitment that I am willing to make? Whatever has come up for you is an example. If you are feeling anxious and overwhelmed, you begin to realize that what needs to happen is to take a time out for yourself. That action step is going to be: What activity can you choose and commit to, to give that time for yourself? Is that going to be five minutes of closing your eyes, going inward through breath or meditation, time spent journaling, reading poetry, or a personal growth book that helps you transcend your current belief system? Work with those thoughts, replacing them with new, positive affirmations, or maybe a daily walk. You can allow that movement to become a meditation helping you to release that anxiety and gain some forward momentum to implement the changes. And if you are struggling with a decision in life, it may be "what choice am I willing to make? What am I willing to settle for? What am I willing to not settle for any longer? What needs to happen here?

You will see that there is so much more to you than the role you convinced yourself that you needed to be. To help you with accepting this change and help you change from negative thought patterns to more positive messages, spend the next few days meditating for about 5 minutes on the affirmation:

"I am transforming into who I am meant to be. I am blooming from a bursting seed to a blossoming flower."

To begin, find a comfortable place to sit and relax. Close your eyes if it is comfortable for you, or allow your gaze to softly fall on something in front of you. Take a deep breath into your lower abdomen, then into your hips, and finally into your lower back. When you are relaxed and in your meditative state, begin repeating *"I am transforming into who I am meant to be. I am blooming from a bursting seed to a blossoming flower."* for several minutes until you feel it become a part of you. Allow it to become something you feel deep inside of you as an innate truth.

Bring your focus back to your heart. Really feeling the calmness, the ability for your heart to speak to you. For you to find the answers within. Feel that love for yourself. The gratitude. And know that you can come back to this place. Any time or place. It is always there. It doesn't have to take meditation. This is a natural part of you that is always there.

Learning to tune into it. Focusing on your heart there. Just envisioning everything is within you there. For you. Just feel what that feels like. Connected to that power within you. That love within your heart that is always there. When it becomes a part of your being, you can bring yourself out of your meditation.

As we come to a close, take note of these changes, in just a moment you can write them down. Integrate them. And take a deep breath. And as you're ready, begin to slowly, slowly, slowly bring yourself back into the present. Slowly opening your eyes, being really gentle with yourself as you open your eyes. The more and more that you practice this, the deeper and deeper that you are going to go. You will begin to find yourself in a really deep place, really gaining a sense of connection that is on. Completely on. So slowly open your eyes, go ahead and take notes on new insights and action steps waiting for you.

When you open your heart to all the opportunities around you, you will notice that you are a radiant being.

PERSONAL SOULWORK 3

To help you complete the 4 steps listed above, to fully realize your true self and silence the nagging voices, work through the following steps one at a time, spending a day or two on each phase.

1. Let go of who you think you need to be.

Part of your first personal Soulwork was to meditate and identify one thing you need to release (the black stone.) Revisit the one thing you want to release that you wrote down during that meditation practice. How are you doing in releasing it? Do you need to take the time to release your feelings related to this release? Take the time now to fully release the emotions related to that item you need to let go, and then ceremonially remove that item from your life. Maybe you burn the paper (in a safe place!) or you bury. Whatever you do, you'll want to physically remove that written statement from your life, just as you are removing it from who you thought you needed to be.

After you complete the process with the original "black stone," continue looking inside yourself to find the things that no longer serve you and write them down. One by one, perform your own ritual of physically releasing these perceptions of the person you are "supposed to be" or "should be."

2. Begin to look into who you are on the inside.

The answer to who you really are is always inside of you. It is just a process of re-discovering this truth. To help you find your inner self, spend time listening to your thoughts and desires in a safe and positive space. Visual meditations will open the space for this inner discovery.

To begin, breathe into your lower abdomen, hips and lower back. When you are relaxed, inhale deeply. On your exhale, imagine opening space inside yourself for your little seed to grow and blossom into a mature flower. On your next inhale, imagine that your little seed is now fully in bloom and you are who you are meant to be. Continue to breathe deeply, appreciating the blossom of your flower. When you have fully realized your internal self and beauty, give thanks to the universe for helping reveal your true self.

Sometimes you'll find words to define who you are and other times it is a feeling. Stay aware so that you keep yourself from falling into the "I'm doing it wrong" or "right" trap. You are transforming in the way that is the best for your authentic self, so take this moment to thank the Universe for guiding you on this path and trust that you will know who you are and what your purpose is when you're ready.

3. Recognize that letting go of who you think you should be opens the door for growth and transformation.

Have you ever noticed that when you clean out a cabinet or drawer in your home, you feel the need to refill it? Do you find that this newly cleared space becomes filled with things quickly? When something is open, nature wants to fill it. This is the same when you clear out the perceptions of how your life "should" be, and open the space to fill it with who you are meant to be. What you'll want to be mindful of during this step is that you fill this space with meaningful thoughts and experiences, and not more distractions that are not leading you through your transformative journey.

Now that you've released all the "clutter" holding you back, jot down in your journal the new opportunities in your life that begin appearing. Identify things that make you happy and feel aligned with your intrinsic purpose. Again, sometimes you can clearly define this information, and sometimes it is more of a feeling. It doesn't matter if it makes sense on paper, just write it down to make sure you are filling your new space with positive, supportive opportunities and thoughts.

4. **Identify the parts of yourself that stay with you no matter what changes are happening around you.**

Sometimes you need to shed the "old" you completely to make room for who you are meant to be. I experienced this when I recognized the drain I felt with my corporate career. Choosing to leave the "successful" and "right" path to discover who I really was empowered me to discover my passion. "Shedding" the part of this façade I was wearing didn't mean I lost all the positive things I learned and discovered along the way. During that time I learned a lot about myself and developed skills that I have taken with me on my current journey. As the saying goes, "don't throw out the champagne with the cork!"

In all experiences, there are positive insights that you can take away from it. The "silver lining." This is the law of wisdom. Look back at the things you listed in the first step; all the things you let go. Take time to think about those experiences or ideas, and write down the positive things they taught you. For example, despite it being a negative influence in your life, you learned how to think out of the box or become more assertive in challenging situations. Take some time to write down the things you have learned that you want to take with you from those experiences, even though those experiences are no longer a part of you.

This is your journey!

JOURNAL PROMPT

"As a society, we are so focused on work and achievement that when we slow down to understand why we do the things we do, we feel a sense of discomfort. It takes practice to own who we are, our value, our worth, our truth."

What are some of the achievements that you experienced, causing you to feel proud or happy, only to feel hollow or uninterested shortly after? Were those related to work that supported your true self or actions taken because it was a societal expectation? Can you determine a time when you accomplished something connected to who you are and your self-worth? Did you feel the same or different? Did the feeling last longer, shorter, or the same?

PART THREE

FIELD GUIDE TO YOUR PROFESSIONAL PURPOSE

CHAPTER EIGHT

LOVE YOUR PROFESSIONAL MESS

"When we know who we are, we create a solid foundation to live a life of meaning and purpose. Clarity is a gift that allows us to realize our full potential and design a life that reflects our greatest hopes and dreams and through living our dreams, we make a difference in the world."
— Robin Emmerich

Over a ten-year span, I've uncovered a common thread in women's professional dreams: to quit their "day job" and start their own business. Many women envision this experience romantically; making their own hours, doing what they "want," not what they are "told," working for hours in coffee shops, sharing ideas with other inspired entrepreneurs.

A while back I had a crazy idea about a new business venture. In addition to my coaching practice and abstract paintings, I wanted to explore the idea of clothing as art. I had spent some time traveling in Florence, Italy and had a revelation that clothing can be a creative and artistic expression as well. I had visited a costume museum there in Florence and the time spent there did not leave me, even after returning to the States. The gallery would not get out of my head. The more I thought about it, the more the idea of printing my abstract art on clothing, specifically yoga pants, became a true vision. Like the costumes in the gallery, my pants could become wearable works of art.

From this vision, my brand, Beauty and the Mess was born.

Well, not that fast…

If only following this path was that easy! The reality is, this vision led to a spark. The spark burned for over a year, while I researched and soul searched. Most of the time, I felt way out of my depth. A simple thought turned into reality is far from easy!

Anytime you need to learn something new, you need to dedicate time to grow and develop into the position. While you may not be breaking out on your own just yet, or you are just trying on another position for size, you need to give yourself the time to learn about an unfamiliar process. When I was exploring this venture I would add things to an expansive to-do list, writing items on there I had no idea about and had never done before. I knew I needed to do them, but did not have the slightest clue on how to approach it. I shut myself in like a caterpillar in a cocoon. I needed to focus and began to avoid friends and family to work. I would spend hours at the coffee shop near my house. Even once, after doing a coaching session at the Texas Women's Conference, I quickly packed up when I was done and disappeared back to my coffee shop "cocoon." Normally I would stay and network with the other participants, but not during this time! I was focused!

But this focus was malleable after several months. I was open to others around me, making small talk and connections with the other regulars in the coffee shop. Many of these people were also entrepreneurs. While they did not all start clothing brands or turn art into wearable items, they did have experience navigating the challenges of doing something new, scary and different of their own success. As I had ideas or challenges, these new friends in my cocoon cheered me on or became a sounding board for my concepts. They offered advice when I needed guidance or even bought me cookies when I needed a push to keep going.

These connections made me realize that to build a business—any type of business—you need help. And you need help from people who can give you relevant and resonant advice.

These connections became my informal team, my *inner circle*. Without their help and advice, it would have probably taken me years to figure it all out. But even with all this amazing help and support, I had to learn a lot of new things. In addition to the unknown, I had a wave of emotions I had to release as well. I felt afraid. I felt unsure of myself. I would feel frustrated, sending the sample back for the 8th time because it still looked nothing like my art, only to get it back again a 9th time incorrect. Without my coffee shop "team," I may not have sent it back for that 10th iteration. They are what made me move forward, even when I was feeling low.

Another thing that I uncovered during my time in the cocoon was the value of my "why." This mission, or purpose, kept me aligned with what I wanted to accomplish. When the process became overwhelming, scary, or difficult, I revisited my purpose to keep me going. For Beauty and the Mess, the mission was embedded in the tagline, "passion over perfection." This message was important to me and I wanted women to be able to receive and give this message all over the world. Remembering this when the "going got tough" kept me going.

Continuing to keep moving forward is paramount to your professional success, whether you are starting or running your own business or succeeding in your established career. Just a tiny step forward, every day, leads you somewhere. You do not need to sprint forward all the time, and when you have no idea what you are doing, sometimes those little steps forward are the most valuable to your success. I realized the power in just moving forward, no matter what, when the day finally came, about 12 months after my idea formed in my mind, when a box arrived on my doorstep. In the box? The first pair of Beauty and the Mess yoga pants printed with my abstract painting exactly as I envisioned it.

Business requires passion and teamwork combined with the guts and stamina to just keep moving forward, even when you sometimes do not know how.

Throughout this chapter, you will have access to tools to help you change your perceptions with your professional development, therefore, changing your reality.

Change Your BCBE

What if I told you that you do not have to feel helpless in a job you dislike? That the feeling of helplessness is holding you back from changing your future?

Part of your perception includes how you see your environment around you. This means that if you can change the way you see your environment, you can change how you feel about it.

I have a formula I rely on for adapting environments. It's called BCBE, and that stands for Belief, Capability, Behavior, and Expectancy. These four elements make up your environment, and if you can change them, you can change your environment.

Your beliefs are the core of who you are, and more importantly, who you think you are. Our beliefs dictate our behavior; if we believe we're not capable of doing something, that is going to affect whether or not we can, in fact, do it—and whether or not we're even willing to try.

In order to change our beliefs, capabilities, and behavior, we also have to shift our expectations. If we expect sadness and misery out of life, we're only going to allow ourselves to experience sadness and misery. Just look at the placebo effect. When you think something is going to make a difference, you can trick your mind into thinking it has. We can do the exact same thing with our environment—by expecting our circumstances to improve, we can see them in a different light.

The four pieces that make up our environment—belief, capability, behavior, and expectations—are all interconnected. You can't change one without changing the other, and all four have to adapt in order to make a difference. As our beliefs change, so do our capabilities. As our capabilities change, we change our behavior—and as our behavior changes, what we expect from our life does as well.

Ultimately, what BCBE teaches us is that more of our environment is in our control than we might at first recognize. Whether it's finding the underlying belief that's affecting our behavior or choosing to see yourself as capable of new skills—like I did, with painting—or understanding that our behavior shapes the response we're getting from the world, so much of the way we experience our environment is in our own minds. And if you can change your mind, you can change your environment—you just have to start by believing it's possible.

If you'd told me a few years ago that I'd be an artist, selling my works and receiving large commission projects, I'd have told you—you were crazy. I didn't believe I was capable of creativity; in fact, before I started painting, I used to say I didn't have a creative bone in my body. But contrary to what online business profile quizzes might tell you, creativity isn't something you have or you don't have. We're all born creative—we just have to allow ourselves the freedom and the confidence to let it out. Whether it's throwing pottery or coming up with your brand's latest marketing campaign, we are all able to engage in creativity—you just have to step up and try.

The first time I painted, I was coming up to the anniversary of my dad's death, around Valentine's Day. I was in a new relationship, and I didn't want the sadness or the fear I still felt from my father's passing to control me. I wanted to find a way to open up, but when my friend, an artist, invited me over to her house to paint, I at first resisted.

"Robin, just come paint with me," she said.

"I don't have one creative bone in my body," I replied.

"Just come over, and pick up a canvas and a few brushes."

Four hours later, I stood in her studio, paint on my hands, the smell of acrylic in the air, staring at the painting I just created. I'd done what my friend had said, picked up a large canvas and some brushes, and showed up at her house, ready to try something new. As I studied my painting, and all I could think was, "Oh my gosh, where did this come from?"

It wasn't until later that I realized that the ability to create had been inside me the whole time, I just had to give myself the freedom to release it—which meant ignoring the fear of "doing it wrong" and failing. Traveling to Italy and an opportunity to see works by the masters inspired me to see the creativity in us all. I believed I had the ability to paint, and this faith in myself opened up a whole new world of art that is now one of my greatest passions.

As I said before, creativity doesn't just have to apply to artwork. A client of mine had always worked for large tech companies, yet as she uncovered her passions, started doing interior design work on the side. As she gained attention for her designs, she gained confidence that not only improved her creative side gig, but also boosted her in her tech job. She started speaking up in meetings more, sharing her ideas—she even cut her hair and started using her clothes as a form of self-expression—and eventually, she moved to a position at one of the most recognizable tech companies in the country.

It's amazing what we can do when we give ourselves freedom to express ourselves. When we have the confidence not to worry about getting our hands messy and coloring outside the lines as we create something great.

Believing in yourself and what you're capable of are nothing if you don't also change your behavior. Your behavior is everything from your thoughts to your words to your body language to your actions.

Take the time now to write down some of the things you tell yourself that you are not capable of accomplishing. Think about actions at work that you feel are beyond your reach or roles you have been told, directly or indirectly, that you are not qualified for. List at least three things you believe you are not capable of below:

1.
2.
3.

Now, reframe what you do not believe you are capable of as if you can do it. Write the statements again, but as if you can do it today. For example, "I am capable of being promoted to a new position and am capable of doing a great job with my skills and abilities."

1.
2.
3.

This activity helps you begin to make a shift in your beliefs and capabilities. But just changing what you believe in and what you are capable of is not enough to make a change. You need to also change your behaviors. Your behavior includes your thoughts, actions, body language, and words. Anything you do as an expression of your beliefs is your behavior. Sometimes when you behave in a way that is disconnected from your true self, you see how it negatively affects your relationships and environment. For example, maybe you are like my client Greg. Greg was studying for the bar exam and spending long lengths of time by himself. He began to feel very disconnected and unhappy with his chosen profession and his relationships. During our time together we uncovered that the separation from others when he spent a lot of time alone, made him feel depressed or negative. When he changed his behavior and connected with the most important things in his life, including his family, he was able to change his feelings towards his environment. When you feel connected to your environment, you can give more of yourself to your role.

The final part of this process means letting go of your expectations. This is the way you can change your beliefs, capabilities, and behavior. For example, if you expect only negative situations to occur, you will only allow yourself to experience these negative situations. Expecting misery and sadness only leads to you experiencing misery and sadness. On the other hand, when you expect something to work out or be positive, you most likely will experience it. This is why there is a placebo effect. When you think the medicine you are taking is designed to help you, it makes a difference, even if what you are taking is not really medicine. You can "trick" your mind into creating positive results. You can shift your expectations about your situation and you will then see how it has improved. You will begin to notice your situation in a different light.

If you are struggling in your current position, take time now to write down how you want your next day or week to go. Focus on defining a positive expectation for that time frame. For example, maybe you have a difficult relationship with your boss or coworker. Frame your expectation as, "On Monday, my boss and I will have a positive conversation and positive workday." Or maybe you do not find satisfaction in your job duties. Frame your expectation like, "This week I will find joy in what I contribute to my office, team, company, or to my role. It will be easy, rewarding, and fun."

Determine what your positive expectation will be and write it down below:

_____

_____

_____

Now take the time to relax into your theta connected state by closing your eyes and breathing into your abdomen, then hips, and finally your lower back. When you are deeply relaxed, repeat your positive expectation several times out loud until you feel it integrate into your mind, heart, body, and spirit. Repeat your expectation until it no longer feels disconnected but rather is a part of your reality.

It's challenging to experience one of these four pieces, belief, capability, behavior, and expectation, without the others. They are interconnected and work together to determine your reality and feelings about your reality. When you begin to change one piece of the puzzle you will change the others. When you are consciously shifting each one of these in the direction of what you want you will see that this adaptation is what makes the difference.

Think of this as a spiral; inside the spiral is the negative space you have been living in. As you begin to adapt your beliefs, you will see your capabilities change. This leads your spiral to move away from the center of negativity. As you spiral outward, your behaviors begin to change. You make choices that are aligned with what is best for you and your values. You continue to spiral away from the negative. Next, your expectations shift, leading you back to adapting your beliefs, then capabilities, and so on. You continue to spiral away from the negative center, continuing to move towards the positive life you expect and are meant to live.

Remember that there is beauty in every situation. What is perceived as a "mess" is often in your highest good. There will be times of conflict, stress, unrest, or boredom in your workplace. Sometimes you will need to work alone or work with a large team. When you understand and use BCBE you will recognize how much of your environment is actually within your control. Your own mind and feelings influence your environment and experiences. Now you can just change your mind and enjoy the change in your environment. You just have to believe it is possible.

I've spoken with my fair share of women who have struggled with figuring out how to have both an amazing career and an amazing relationship. What I often find to be the case, however, is that they're trying to both be an awesome colleague, boss, career woman while simultaneously swiping right on every man in sight.

My advice is: one thing at a time. Figure out what you want out of life and let your own clarity find someone to share it with.

I've followed this advice in my own life. Several years ago, I was dating a guy who I felt was actually pretty selfish. Somehow we always ended up doing what he wanted to do, and I felt like I—and my interests—had taken a back seat in the whole relationship. I was sharing this with a mentor when it dawned on me: The reason we never did anything I wanted was that I wasn't willing to speak up and say what that was. I didn't know myself—my hopes or my dreams—well enough to bring that passion into a relationship. I ended up focusing on my goals, personal and professional. Only after I'd improved my relationship with myself, fully understanding my wants and needs, was I able to have strong relationships with others.

In order to attract the right kind of people, we have to be confident in who we are and what we want. A friend of mine, Allison, was applying for her dream job. She'd been struggling with self-doubt in her current role. She felt unqualified for the kind of job she wanted, yet I was able to show her that it had nothing to do with her qualifications, just her confidence. Once she understood that, she was able to go after the job she really wanted.

Fast forward several months, and she not only landed her dream job, but she's thriving in it. She's jet-setting around the world working on cool projects, making enough to buy her downtown condo, and is enjoying more autonomy than she's ever had in a job. Now that she's figured out her career, Allison is looking around and asking, Now who do I share this with?

I find that many women tend to be in a panic about being single, even if they're crushing it in their careers. They think that all the time they spent focusing on themselves and their goals is time wasted, the time they could have spent nurturing a relationship. I disagree. By focusing on their own growth and development, they're going to attract the kind of men who want to see them successful and thriving—the kind of men who will respect their accomplishments and that they can respect in return. What I don't agree with is the myth that "You have to be single to find yourself." Focusing on your growth is not about making a statement that checks off the box "I am single, building an empire". This is just another form of control.

Authentic growth is taking the steps to get clear on who you are and creating space in your life to attract it. That may equate to a day, a month or a year.

This goes for your career as well. One woman, I worked with went from making $30,000 to making $150,000 in less than one year. And like I've seen it happen time and time again, just as she was on top of the world in her personal development, a man walked into her life. The only issue was, she didn't have time for a relationship—she worked late every day and every weekend to earn that $150,000 salary. She ultimately decided that it was worth cutting back on her career to make room for a relationship. She's not back to making $30,000 a year through—all that time she spent investing in herself has made it possible for her to attract both an amazing guy and a well-paying (though less demanding) job. Her heart is fulfilled and they just moved into their first home together with marriage and family in their future.

Where are you at in your relationship, career, and personal development? I believe we go through seasons in each area, and while we can have it all, that doesn't mean we have to get it all right at the same time.

Now is a beautiful time for new beginnings.

Start by reflecting on your BCBE, working towards loving yourself and being your biggest cheerleader as you pursue your goals—let that love enhance your current relationship or let the person who's going to cheer alongside you find you.

CHAPTER NINE

THE TRUTH ABOUT INTUITION

"Do you know what the music is saying?
Come to follow me and you will find the way.
Your mistakes can also lead you to the Truth.
When you ask, the answer will be given."

– Rumi

As you have learned from the previous chapter, your beliefs, capabilities, behaviors, and expectations are powerful internal forces that can determine your success and happiness in your career. Sometimes, you feel unsettled when you have been in the same position for a while, even though you are comfortable with your job requirements. Sometimes you feel like you are on autopilot. Other times you question if what you are doing is making a difference or if it matters. You lack fulfillment in your job.

At this point, many people cut their ties and run to the next opportunity. They decide that everything is not going well and their skin is practically crawling with the urge to get out, now. They have lost the passion for their job and are certain it exists, but not where they are at now.

That may describe you to a "T." You may think, "Yes! I did the BCBE and still find it hard to feel fulfilled in my job." And you may be thinking you should stop right now and begin working on your resume because I understand how you feel so well that it must be time to go looking for greener pastures. PAUSE right now and take a deep breath. It's not about how to find something else out there; it's about how to find *the something* in your heart.

You have the ability to change your mind, body, and spirit. You have this innate power; it is your birthright! To begin your transformation, it was important that you started breaking free from your perceived limitations. Releasing the blocks that held you back and developing new tools to help you move forward opened a whole new path. When you change your beliefs, you change your behavior, and in turn, change the entire course of your existence.

It is often fear that limits your beliefs. These fears are linked to previous experiences and emotions and limit your true potential. To rise above these, we tap into the subconscious and access the truth. Your true beliefs develop new behaviors. These new behaviors take time to adapt, which is why you may experience these up's and down's. Sticking with them, or as we say, going back to the basics, will move you to a higher level. And when you begin to doubt, and fear slithers its way back into your mind, recognize that it is only there to draw you closer to your truth. Practice letting go. Dr. Long has taught me how our subconscious, or the "unthinking" mind, has unlimited access to universal knowledge. I've witnessed it in hundreds of people. You already contain all the wisdom and energy necessary to soar, if you just see the truth of your conscious mind and let your heart connect with your subconscious.

This understanding can open up a whole new way to look at your life. Think about it as if things no longer "happen" to you, but rather are "caused" by you. Your beliefs determine your actions, which are developed by your conscious or subconscious. As you connect more to this universal wisdom, you have the opportunity to create success, vitality, and joy in your own life. You no longer have to "wait" for it to come to you! To help you identify a truth versus a blurred false understanding (often the result of fear), you can learn from the universal laws. This understanding helps you clarify your vision, like putting glasses on after needing them for so long.

I always recommend going back to basics.

1. What is your mind saying?
2. Ask your higher power, "Is it in my highest good..."
3. Can you accept your inner truth? Rejecting your truth is betraying yourself. That is the true form of betrayal.
4. Tune into your heart. What does your heart want?
5. Can you let go of your expectations and follow the path of the heart? This is where your journaling is helpful. I recommend that you let yourself draw out your desires as

well. Use colorful pencils. Let your inner child show you the way to your desires.

You know the feeling: you've been at your job for long enough that you're comfortable with your job requirements, but nonetheless, you feel unsettled. Maybe tension has started to develop between you and your coworkers, or perhaps you feel like you're not moving up the ladder the way you planned. Now, just when you've gotten in the groove at your company, you're starting to dream about moving on. You're unhappy with a few things about your job that start to feel like *everything* about your job, and your skin is practically crawling with an urge to get out, now. You know you're meant to do more, but just don't know what that is.

This feeling hit me a few years ago, when I was working as division manager in the staffing field. I felt like I could feel my life ticking away, like nothing I was doing *mattered*. In reality, I was connecting people to entirely new careers. Opening doors for success. The problem was that I could do the job in my sleep—I was on autopilot. I felt a lack of fulfillment in my day-to-day life. While it sounds silly to complain about work being "too easy," I wasn't happy feeling *that* impassioned by my job.

That's when I sought out a mentor, a woman who could help me get to the core of what I really wanted. She didn't let me just up and quit my job immediately, however; we spent a long time getting to the heart of *why* I was unhappy.

What I discovered was that this job reflected where I was spiritually. I didn't have a clear vision of who I was and what I wanted. Yes, I had taken the Myer-Briggs personality test, but I had no idea of my purpose and how I could contribute to the world in a way that fulfilled me as well. My company culture did not fit my values and I had more expertise with nowhere to go.

Start by asking yourself: what is it about myself that is holding me back? Identifying the underlying issue is the first step in any job—or any relationship, for that matter—in deciding whether it's time to stay or go. Not only will you be able to make a more educated decision on your current job, but you'll also be prepared to identify the job that will make you happier in the future and navigate the path to achieving it. Let yourself dream big on what you really want and visualize achieving that dream.

Like the previous chapter, I worked with mentors along the way. Sometimes they fill a spot just for the time being and other times they stay with you for long periods of time. Either way, these are the people you can look up to and talk to about the positive and negative feelings and experiences you are encountering. Take time to think of the people around you that you could go to as a mentor. They may be a co-worker, boss, friend, neighbor, or the guy in the coffee shop who always offers sage advice when you need it. Write down their name and why you consider them a mentor to you:

Name:

_____

Mentorship Role:

_____

Name:

_____

Mentorship Role:

_____

Name:

_____

Mentorship Role:

_____

It is ok if you have just one name listed above. This is not about the number of mentors in your life, it is about the quality of support and advice they offer to you. If you have no names listed above, that is ok, too! This just means it's time to start putting yourself out there, looking for people that you admire and respect. Look for the people that are doing what you want to be doing, and reach out to them. Ask them for help; share with them your experiences and feelings. Find at least one person you can turn to in times of need.

When I met with my mentor, she helped me dig under the surface of my unhappiness and discontent. I realized that the unfulfillment in my job was a reflection of my unfulfilled spirituality. Or, to put it another way, it reflected how unattached I was to who I was and what I wanted. This uncertainty in myself made me uncertain about everything. I had no idea how I could offer something with substance to the world in a way that also fulfilled my soul. Before I could make a move, I needed to get on the right page. I needed to figure out who I was and what I wanted before I made a move.

Here is the problem with job-hopping because you are unhappy with your position or where you are in your company; your problems go with you. Leaving does not solve a thing. If you change jobs now, in a few months, you will be unhappy again. The pattern continues to repeat itself. Then what will you do?

The answer: you need to dig deeper instead of stopping at the statement, "I am unhappy with my job." The solution is in the core of the problem. If you are in this place in your career, take the time to name the things you are dissatisfied with. Take the time now to write down the things that are continuing to be an issue, even after you go through the BCBE steps:

_____

_____

_____

After listing the various issues you are facing, look for a pattern. Is there something that seems to trigger your unhappiness? Maybe it is a situation, person, activity, or culture that makes you unsettled and unsatisfied. Look for what "strings" your situations together. Review what you wrote above and list the pattern or patterns below:

_____

_____

_____

Now, look at the information you listed above. Does the pattern seem to run like a vein through more than just your professional life? Is it affecting different areas of your life as well? This is how powerful and deep-rooted discontent can run.

How many times have you or someone you have known applied to a job with a similar company for a similar position? It would be a lateral move, landing a job in something similar in hopes it would change everything.

One of my friends told me she was doing this, frantically searching for a new job just like the one she had, but just with another company. I talked with her about why she wanted to make a lateral move and together we began to uncover her root cause of unhappiness. She chose to continue her pattern because at the heart of it all she doubted her qualifications and skills to be able to excel in her dream job at her dream company. In fact, she had all the qualifications and skills to be able to do the job and fulfill the role at that company, but it was her self-doubt that stopped her. This self-doubt crept into every role, holding her back from ever settling comfortably into her positions.

After we uncovered this core issue, I asked her to hit pause on the frenzied job search. Instead, I guided her to spend a full 24-hours to focus and envision herself being offered, accepted, and succeeding in the role at her dream company. My intent was not to have her leave her current role just to start again in another similar situation. She would be just recreating her current unhappy situation all over again. Instead, I wanted her to envision her next career move.

Now that you have identified the pattern that is holding you back, switch gears and start imagining what it is that you want. What would your dream company and dream job look like? How would this position and company make you happy?

Spend time, maybe throughout a full day, writing down your answers below:

_____

_____

_____

If you don't know what your dream job or dream company is, spend a few moments to a few days looking for this information. Find what situation would make you happy and write it down above.

And just like I guided my friend, now take the time to think about all the things that you feel are holding you back from achieving it:

_____

_____

_____

Chances are that you didn't have any trouble writing down all the things you had an issue with or were dissatisfied with, and you probably did not have a problem writing down all the things stopping you from achieving your goals, but writing down what will make you happy is a bit harder. It is even harder to honestly look at how you are self-sabotaging your success.

After my friend took the day to reflect, she interviewed for a position she felt excited about and accepted the offer when it was offered to her. While she was excited to accept the advanced position, what was most important was that she had gained clarity on what job satisfaction looked like for her. She accepted the position because she knew it would fulfill her internally.

Now that you have reflected on your goals and how you could be self-sabotaging your success, now you can define what your job satisfaction will look like for yourself. Maybe during this self-revelation, you will uncover that your current role or current company can offer you this satisfaction or maybe it will reveal that it cannot. Create the space for your decision to stay in your role or leave to be made from a true understanding of what you want. Allow yourself to seek support from a mentor.

Having these tools in your toolbox means you can make educated decisions about your current job and also be prepared to identify the job that will make you happier in the future. They will also help you identify the path on how you can achieve it. Let yourself dream big on what you really want and visualize achieving that dream!

Connect To Your Intuition

For years I climbed the corporate ladder. I was at the top of the company. I was in a relationship with the "perfect match," according to my girlfriends. I was in the best physical shape of my life. When people looked at me, I appeared to have it all. And, at the time, I thought I did. It was not until I let my attention slip from driving and I hit a guardrail that I began my journey to connecting back with my intuition.

My accident woke me up through the pain. It was a minor accident, but the pain in my back was unbearable. The pain was frustrating; I felt like my world was crumbling. I was seeing my acupuncturist who recommended I see a counselor. He explained that my pain could be linked with other trauma, such as my father's death ten years earlier. I doubted his reasoning, but I did begin to meet with my spiritual director every week.

During my sessions, I had to examine my life from the inside out. My "perfect" life began to melt away. During this time, I uncovered that I no longer knew who I was. I did not know what I wanted. I had no idea how to be truly happy. Before, all I focused on were others and external circumstances. I focused on keeping my boyfriend who was never available. I focused on my friend who was marrying an alcoholic. I focused on my mom and sister who always determined what was best for me. I focused on my boss who needed me to fill three different roles.

While I may have looked like I had it all, and while I felt like I was succeeding, I was really just a disaster on the inside. I began working with Dr. Coletta Long. This is how I discovered how deeply my father's death had affected my subconscious. This then led to the discovery that I could live the life that I truly wanted and not just what my brain, and society said I should want. In time, I transformed every aspect of my life. It started with my career and then looking at my relationship. Again, what you change in one area will help you create change in the other.

You can gain this clarity when you understand how your mind works. Remember that your subconscious is connected to your intuition, and it is your conscious mind that tells you what the world thinks you need. It sends you messages like, "no, you do not deserve that promotion." Or "do not even bother looking for your dream job." These thoughts are disconnected from your true desires. Your intuition and subconscious, on the other hand, are tied to them. When you understand and identify the difference between the two you can decipher the messages of your brain.

Your conscious mind will complicate your life with loud, misleading stories. When you learn to let go of these stories and quiet the noise, you can connect your mind and heart. You can experience the transformation you are looking for. My favorite way to connect with your true desires is to find a quiet place to sit for about five minutes. Take a deep breath, relax your body and mind, and set your intention on listening to your heart. Allow your heart to talk to you, asking your mind to step aside so you can listen to what your heart is saying. Answer for yourself, what needs to happen so you can have a happy, full, and successful career? Or, more broadly, what needs to happen so you can experience happiness, fulfillment, and success?

Cultivate trust. Let this deep question of the soul reveal itself to you in the perfect timing.

PROFESSIONAL SOULWORK 2

As you have discovered, you will begin to notice more and more: what people, what places, what experiences, what moments of today were really there as an opportunity to see the truth and begin to see from the place of your heart, from a connection to the mind, body, and spirit.

Questions to ask yourself:

1. Where do I get excited in my life?
2. What really turns me on and fuels me?
3. How do I feel most free in my life? What makes me feel free? What makes me feel constricted? What do I want to attract in my life that feels like I am really on purpose?

Notice what fuels you rather than what exhausts you. As you begin to connect to more of that, you are going to begin to feel it. So again take 5 minutes before bed to really reflect and begin to connect more to yourself. As you gain momentum, you will discover more authentic connections with others and more happiness in your life.

JOURNAL PROMPT

"Your conscious mind will complicate your life with loud, misleading stories. When you learn to let go of these stories and quiet the noise, you can connect your mind and heart. You can experience the transformation you are looking for."

Think about a "loud" story that your mind tells you over and over again. Write down this illusion that you have convinced yourself is real. Now imagine if your mind told you a different story. Imagine if you heard the opposite over and over again. What would that story sound like? Rewrite your example into something that is supporting and encouraging you rather than disconnecting you from your truth.

PART FOUR

CONNECTING THE PIECES

APPRECIATING THE JOURNEY

Stop.
Do not move forward without doing something fun to celebrate YOU!

Life is meant to be celebrated. When you love the mess, you are appreciating who you are and everything around you! You know and trust that the events in your life are for you.

Take time now to look back: How did you feel at the beginning of this journey? What is the reality you are living in now?

Think about the things that once held you back from accomplishing your desires. Maybe it was a lack of understanding of what you really wanted, looking at others for your insight, or having the confidence to listen to your intuition. You know you have the tools to find that clarity. No matter where you are at, you are getting closer to your truth. I will share a little insight on this; sometimes we are meant to be "veiled" to experience the growth needed to move forward. Your humanity will uncover your saboteur archetype or simply pull you back into conscious-mind cloudiness. That is normal! As I mentioned, there is an ebb and flow to life. You now have tools and experience to overcome adversity and tune into the heart of the matter.

And now that you know you have the tools, and the "veil" has been or has begun to lift, you can face the opportunity in front of you. But as Carl Jung explains, there are universal archetypes, or collective and universal behaviors that we all experience, and one of them is the "saboteur." I was conscious of my inner saboteur when I was standing in line at the LA Convention Center in 2019. Waiting to walk across the hot coals of fire during Tony Robbins' Unleash the Power Within event, I had to recognize and listen to my inner voice that was leading me.

Tony teaches you how to conquer the fear every step of the way. I watched person after person walk across the fire and celebrate their power like nothing I have ever seen before. I also saw some turn around at the face of uncertainty and make their way back inside. Those that celebrated their empowerment screamed with a delight that I have never heard in my life. When it was my turn to step up to the fire, I repeated my intention and listened to my intuition. I knew it was my time. There was no turning back. I was conscious of my inner saboteur and had I been led to turn around, I would have trusted that and accepted it. That simply wasn't where I was at. I knew my intention, Tony fully prepared us, and I was ready.

Words can't describe the sense of power and joy within me after I walked across that fire. My life will never be the same. I don't have all the answers to what that means, and at the same time, I can share that's simply not how life works. Life is fully lived when you can take one step and let the next unfold. That step may be looking at potential job opportunities, going on a date, or walking on fire. All that matters is that you take one step.

Life is a series of twists and turns, guided by your past and inspired by your future. Losing sight of the present and the miracles around you will steer you off your path. Every now and then, close your eyes and trust that you are going in the direction you need to go. Believe that the Universe is guiding you down the river of life towards the sights you need to see and the people you need to meet. You will experience the things you are meant to experience if you paddle along the current of your true self. It is when you beat back against this current, battle your subconscious connection, and try to change the course of life, that you experience frustration, sadness, and worse.

My hope in writing this book is for you to have gained a few keys to remember each and every day; first, that you have the power to let go of the emotions that are holding you back from experiencing your life fully. It's not about letting go of the memory of something or someone, it's about letting go of the emotions that are causing you to experience events in your life that are not in alignment with who you are. Second, you have more control over your environment than you may think. You can change your perceptions to change your reality. And finally, you have the ability to connect to your intuition and live a meaningful life by using tools to bring yourself back to you.

Remember, life is leading you in the right direction. The Universe is holding your hand and walking you down your life path. Rather than resisting, close your eyes and allow yourself to be led. Love the mess and let the beauty unfold...

YOUR FINAL SOULWORK—FOR NOW!

Whether you chose to explore your personal and intimate relationships or chose to focus on your professional development, you noticed change outside of what you were seeking. Maybe when you were focused on deepening your relationship with your partner or attracting a new relationship, you suddenly received a promotion or a breakthrough at work you've been working towards. Or maybe you were committed to finding satisfaction in your career and then found a new partner you feel deeply connected with.

The truth is, your life is not meant to be compartmentalized. You cannot change one area without affecting the other. You cannot only develop your personal life and leave your professional life alone and vice versa. You are an interconnected being, and the actions you take influence everything in your life. Once you understand this, there is so much freedom available to you! The tools in this book are here to help you transform your life for the better. My mentor always recommended the mantra, "Every day in every way, my life is getting better and better."

During your exploration throughout this book, when you had to choose a side, personal or professional, I had you embark on one final Soulwork prelude. You explored and developed one area of your life, but are now able to recognize the impact your decisions have had on your entire life. Now, for your final Soulwork, take the time to go back and explore the chapters you have not yet followed. Explore your professional journey if you followed the personal path, or dive into your personal arena if you stuck to the professional earlier. Consider how the tools in each of the chapters apply to all situations you encounter rather than just the examples provided in these pages.

Your tools are now exposed here for you to use, over and over again. You have a series of steps and resources to help you navigate any challenges so that you can continue to live your most authentic, happy life. Come back to your pages when you want to release an emotional block. Connect to your soul and intuition by following the BCBE method. This is your guide to stay connected to yourself. It is your secret weapon to success, happiness, and connectivity (ok, maybe not so secret anymore!).

I am so grateful and honored to guide you into your mind, heart, emotional reset and journey to love the mess; the true you.

Now that you can touch this truth, it is up to you to get up, get going, and live the life that you are meant to live.

And live it with love in your heart.

Bibliography

Neimark, J. (1995, January 1). It's Magical, It's Malleable, It's... Memory. *Psychology Today* .

I met Robin at a magazine launch party about 7 years ago, and—as with all pivotal moments in life—our "chance encounter" turned out to be divine timing more than coincidence.

Outwardly, I was living life as a successful, young entrepreneur. My business was thriving, delivering high value, gaining great publicity, and providing meaningful work for others. However, if you were to have looked over my shoulder at the time, you might have noticed a much darker picture: 60 – 80hr workweeks, a nonexistent love life, and an incessant drive to push harder to prove my worth.

Before I met Robin, I'd participated in several business programs and incubators. And while each equipped me with new tools, concepts and strategies, they overlooked the deep, transformative work that needed to take place for me to truly find peace, love and fulfillment.

When I met Robin, I'd never heard the term "transformational coach," and certainly had no idea I needed one! But she told me she'd help me work less and love more, and I thought, "Sure! Let's give it a shot."

Working with Robin cracked me open spiritually. Her deep, transformative work not only shifted my mindset but also began exposing deep core wounds that had created my workaholic lifestyle.

I realized that, for too long, I'd shut off my heart and intuition and was making decisions based on what I thought would be best rather than what I felt would be best. With Robin's help, I began to see the difference and was catapulted into a new way of being that embraced my heart, my gut and my spirituality.

These shifts not only improved my quality of life, but they also positively impacted my business, propelling me to new successes and opportunities I otherwise wouldn't have known were possible. Today, I still love business strategy, and learning about new tools and concepts. I also know on a deep level that without inner growth, outward growth will always be a struggle.

Without Robin, I may not have married my husband or discovered my own passion for coaching and advising

entrepreneurial women. I'm so grateful Robin and I crossed paths when we did. Working with her changed my life!
— RACHEL BROWNLOW LUND, BUSINESS GROWTH
COACH + SPEAKER | ME2LEAD

At 31 I found myself a year post divorce— generally content yet with a lingering feeling I was missing something. My career while stable with ample room for growth did not excite me. I was three years invested and another two with graduate school. I knew if I was going to follow my heart and have meaningful work in line with my passion the time was now— or never. Yet I had no idea where to start or what my passion even was.

Then I met Robin Emmerich, I took her course on creativity and it shifted the entirety of my life. Through her course and coaching I removed blocks, limitations and thought patterns that limited my true potential. I started saying yes to the small soft whisper of my intuition and heart's desire. The techniques and tools I learned guided me to a world of possibility. I took a spontaneous trip to Costa Rica, enrolled in art classes and soon discovered my passion as a metal-smith jeweler. A year later, I was working as an apprentice jeweler and the following year ended up relocating across the country to gain more metal-smithing experience before finally landing my dream job as a goldsmith working with estate jewelry. My life continues to expand in new and exciting ways I hadn't imagined. Robin's guidance, tools, and insights have been vital in creating a life I love!
— RORY G.

Made in the USA
Monee, IL
17 August 2020